D1486148

THE SOCIAL HISTORY OF EDUCATION

GENERAL EDITOR: VICTOR E. NEUBURG

Second Series — No. 8

SCHOOL ECONOMY

THE SOCIAL HISTORY OF EDUCATION

General Editor: Victor E. Neuburg

Second Series

SCHOOL ECONOMY

A Practical Book on

THE BEST MODES OF ESTABLISHING
AND TEACHING SCHOOLS

And of Making them Thoroughly Useful to the
Working Classes by Means of

Moral and Industrial Training

BY

JELINGER SYMONS

REPRINTS OF ECONOMIC CLASSICS

Augustus M. Kelley · Publishers
NEW YORK 1971

Published by

WOBURN BOOKS LIMITED

10 WOBURN WALK, LONDON WC1 0JL

First edition   1852
New impression   1971

ISBN 7130 0017 1

Published in the U. S. A. by

AUGUSTUS M. KELLEY, PUBLISHERS

Clifton, New Jersey

Printed in Great Britain by Clarke, Doble & Brendon Ltd.
Plymouth and London

SCHOOL ECONOMY:

A PRACTICAL BOOK

ON THE

BEST MODES OF ESTABLISHING AND TEACHING

SCHOOLS,

AND OF MAKING THEM THOROUGHLY USEFUL
TO THE WORKING CLASSES

BY MEANS OF

MORAL AND INDUSTRIAL TRAINING.

BY

JELINGER SYMONS, A.B.

LONDON:
JOHN W. PARKER AND SON, WEST STRAND.
MDCCCLII.

TO THE

VERY REVEREND RICHARD DAWES, M.A.

DEAN OF HEREFORD.

MY DEAR SIR,

I WISH I could think this little book in the least degree
worthy of your sanction. It may, however, serve as
a means of expressing the gratitude which I, and all
friends of real education feel to you, as the exponent of the
best mode of teaching the poor, and of adapting schools
to the wants of life. If this revolution in the prevailing
system should come to pass, it will be owing to you more
than to any one else.

This work is an humble attempt to give practical furtherance to the principles you have laid down. I can truly
say, that a very extensive inspection of schools of all kinds,
at home and abroad, for twenty years, though it has abun-
dantly disclosed defects, has failed to give me the same
insight into remedies that I have derived from the 'hints,'
both written and oral, which I owe to your public zeal and
private friendship. Please to accept this slight tribute of
high esteem from

Yours faithfully and respectfully,

JELINGER SYMONS.

The Vineyard, near Hereford,
  May 1, 1852.

ADVERTISEMENT.

It may be expedient to guard against the mistake, that in the expression of my own views in this book, I am in any degree expressing those of the Committee of Council on Education ; or that their lordships are in the remotest way compromised by its contents. As an Inspector of schools, it is just possible that such a mis-impression might arise. I have, on the contrary, refrained from seeking any other sources of information than such as were equally open to others. So far have I carried this, that I have to correct an error, into which I might not otherwise have fallen, in the statement at page 5, that 'in church schools, aided by grants, care is taken (by the Committee of Council) that dissenters' children may be educated, and at the same time exempted from instruction in the distinctive doctrines and catechism of the Church.' It is not exactly so ; though this system is often recommended to, and adopted by, the promoters and managers of such schools.

J. S.

CONTENTS.

PART THE FIRST.

CHAP. I. *How to Start and Maintain Schools.*

CHAP. II. *Need of Better Schools.*

CHAP. III. *How to make Schools thoroughly useful for Poor Children.*

PART THE SECOND.

CHAP. I. *The Building and Organization of Schools.*

Chap. V. *Religious Education and Moral Training.*

Chap. VI. *School Teachers.*

PART THE THIRD.

CHAP. I. *Industrial Training.*

CHAP. II. *The School Farm.*

LIST OF APPENDICES.

PART THE FIRST.

CHAPTER I.

How to Start and Maintain Schools.

THE subject of Schools for the people suggests two great questions: first, how best to establish and maintain them; and, secondly, what sort of schools they should be. Although this work is intended chiefly to aid this last consideration, and that after a very practical fashion, it is, notwithstanding, expedient to clear one's way through those restless controversies and bootless feuds, which beset the first of these questions, and obstruct the second.

Every good man would probably desire that each class or denomination of Christians, in an enlightened country like this, should educate its own poor; or, better still, that its own poor should educate themselves. The State, in such a case, would have no call upon it to interfere in the matter, unless, indeed, in behalf of the pauper or criminal classes, who, as waifs of the State, must be cared for by its Government, and by common consent fall under its tutelage. But, unhappily, our moral shortcomings stand in sad contrast with our physical achievements, and, as a people, we do not educate our poor; and it is now a very generally admitted fact, that if their education is to depend on voluntary effort and individual benevolence, they will, for the most part, not be educated at all. The failures of the voluntary principle are too numerous, signal, and decisive, to leave this a matter of question by any unbiassed man acquainted with the facts. It becomes, therefore, a matter of simple alternative, either to have the poor educated by public means, or to sacrifice their education to a stubborn preference of what is impracticable. The good sense of Dissenters already largely preponderates in favour of doing that by public money which will not be done by private purses. As to a violation of the rights of conscience by such a system, on the pretext that it is making one creed pay for the religious instruction of another, it is obvious that such can alone result from the partial rejection, and not from the general acceptance, of aid from the fund to which all contribute. The evil objected to is, in fact, the result of the objection. If the Churchman and Dissenter severally receive as much from the fund for the payment of grants to schools as they contribute to it, no support is given by one to the other; but if either of them refuse to receive his share of the benefit, the fault is his own, and the alleged injustice entirely of his own creation. The difficulty on this score is not worthy of consideration by Parliament or the country, and ought not to stand for a moment in the way of effective State aid to schools for the poor on the most liberal and catholic scale.

Nevertheless, partly in deference to this objection, it is proposed to dissever religious from secular instruction, and to apply State grants only to the latter. In other words, to give the husk without the kernel.

If our education is to be education at all, it must moralize and Christianize. It must educate the heart as well as the head and hand; and, if so, what possible means is there of doing this without religion, or of teaching religion without the Bible? No man of sense wishes to degrade the Bible into a mere reading or class book; but unless it be interwoven with all primary teaching, and associated in the child's mind with every duty he learns, as the essence by which his moral being is to be inspired and guided, there can be little security for the right use of mental instruction—a power more likely to be wielded for evil than for good, if unaccompanied by the moral principle which can alone render it a blessing to the scholar and a boon to society.

Some of the advocates of a secular system of education say that they desire to incorporate a high moral philosophy with their temporal teaching. That is to say, they would give the stream without the source. Their scholars may learn Christianity, so long as they be not taught of Christ! They may be schooled in the duties of charity, but much in the way in which they might learn them from Pagan ethics; for they are not to drink in the living spirit in all the fulness of that glorious manifestation of love in the life and death of the Redeemer, as told by the Evangelists. They may perchance hear of God, but not through the revelation of Himself which He has expressly provided for their instruction. His omnipresence, justice, truth, loving-kindness, mercy, and omnipotence, they may gather dimly and deviously through the pages of human science, or the mouths of human teachers; but from the glowing words of that wondrous book inspired by God, in which His attributes are divinely developed, they may not learn them! In such schools, the Bible would be more completely excluded than in the most rigid of the Romish seminaries. Dr. Hook, in his letter to the Bishop of St. David's, thus ably denounces this grave error :—

Upon investigating the subject, we find that a notion prevails among careless people, that religion may be treated as either general or special : special religion is doctrinal, and general religion is some system of morals, which, being divested of all doctrine, looks so like no religion at all, that religious persons at once perceive, that when people talk of an education based on such a religion, they seek to deceive themselves as well as us, and utter a falsehood.

Now all really Christian persons must stand opposed to any system of education which, being professedly based upon this general religion, which is no religion, will in fact unchristianize this country. To separate the morality of the Gospel from the doctrines of the Gospel, every one who knows what the Gospel is, knows to be impossible. The doctrines of grace and of good works are so interwoven that they must stand or fall together. Faith and works, doctrine and morality, are like body and soul; the pretended mother may be willing to divide them; they who know what the Gospel is, like the true mother before the throne of Solomon, will suffer any affliction before they will consent to it.   Satan could devise no scheme for the extirpation of Christianity more crafty or more sure than this, which would substitute a system of morals for religion.   The generality of mankind content themselves always with the lowest degree of religion, which will silence their conscience and aid their self-deception. They desire to believe as little as they may without peril to their souls, and to do only what the majority of their neighbours say they must.   On this general religion, which is no religion—on this semblance of religion, this shadow put for the substance, the majority of the people of England will, under such a system of education, be taught to rest as sufficient.

In defence of a system thus practically irreligious, we are told that the children will receive religious instruction at home and elsewhere, at the hands of their parents or friends. To this assertion, a direct contradiction is the best and truest answer.   The parents and friends of those children who need religious instruction the most, are the very last persons fit or likely to give it ; and to expect it from them, or to believe that such children will seek it elsewhere for themselves, is a mischievous delusion.   If these poor children, whose present minds and morals most need religious instruction, do not obtain it at our schools, they will have it nowhere.

The difficulties in the way of giving effectual religious teaching in schools for the poor, aided by public grants, have been vastly exaggerated, if not wholly created, by a sectarian monomania, which, though not very prevalent, is sufficiently noisy and restless to impair the peacefulness and effectiveness with which the general body of Churchmen and Dissenters would perhaps have otherwise laboured to educate their poor.   It has, moreover, spoiled many efforts, and prevented the establishment of many schools. Judging from its practical working, where fairly trusted and fully tried, it is probable that the present system, if its operation were enlarged by more liberal grants, would answer every purpose as regards the establishment and maintenance of schools.   The Church of England has received the largest part of the grants already made, nor is it either natural or desirable that it should be otherwise.   In the first place, it is the established religion of the country. It is also undeniable, that of all classes and denominations of men, our clergy have been pre-eminent in their zealous and noble efforts to advance the education of the poor. The rights of conscience, and the privileges of Dissenters, have been nevertheless carefully provided for, not only by the precautions taken, that in Church schools, aided by public grants, their children may be educated, and at the same time exempted from instruction in the distinctive doctrines and catechism of the Church, which would clash with their own religious persuasions, but they are themselves entitled to grants for their own schools, and some excellent ones have been so established, in connexion with the British and Foreign and Wesleyan societies.   This system, so far from requiring an organic change, may be said to have worked well enough to render any extensive alteration in its principle a speculation of very questionable expediency.   The condition of the grants, viz., that of a proportionate amount of local aid and contribution, is, perhaps, better calculated than any other system would be to secure the vitality of that interest in the school, on the part of its promoters, which is often essential, and always conducive to its success.   To substitute for this, the compulsory superintendence which a system of schools supported by local rates would necessitate, might not prove equally beneficial.   Assuredly, the difficult and delicate task of duly organizing and managing schools admits of no comparison, and has no analogy, with that of the relief of pauperism and the local administration of the Poor Laws.

The chances are, that anything approaching to a similar mode of superintending or conducting schools for the poor, would entirely defeat their object.

Whilst education for the poor cannot subsist on voluntary effort alone, neither can State efforts suffice without voluntary co-operation. For it is essential to the good government and successful teaching of schools for the poor, that local interest in their welfare should foster and animate them. There is no surer way to secure this, than by making those from whom such interest must flow contribute to its object. The proportion in which this is done is comparatively immaterial, so long as it *be* done. The school is thenceforth *ours*, not *others';* and there is magic in the possessive pronoun, where the question is how to engender an enduring and active sympathy.

A politic and not an unworthy consideration in support of the present system, is presented by the sectarian tendency of that religious feeling among us, which almost necessarily inspires our educational efforts. It is questionable how far it is wise or just to the interests of the uneducated poor to run counter to so powerful a principle. The only systematized effort to establish schools apart from religious principles, has certainly met with significant indifference from the country at large. Scarcely any such exist; and what is more remarkable is, the predominance of some one religious body or sect in nearly every school in which religion is taught. In any, above the standard of mere dame schools, there is very little blending of denominations. But few Church children attend the British or Dissenting schools, whilst those of the Establishment are very partially attended by any but its own children. The British and Foreign are essentially Dissenting schools; nor is this all, for however unsectarian the articles of their constitution, one denomination usually predominates in, if it does not monopolise, the management. However true it is, therefore, that these schools are theoretically catholic, they are often practically sectarian. This state of things is not only the natural growth and produce, but it has been part and parcel of all religious realities among us for three centuries past. Independence of judgment, diversity of creed, and sincerity of faith, have necessarily produced it; less, perhaps, as a result of the Reformation (which they rather caused), than of that English love of free judgment which is incarnate in us. Our national mind is, moreover, peculiar; and though our convictions are usually sincere, even when passive, they are seldom earnest until animated by antagonism; and this characteristic pertains peculiarly to our religious opinions. It is, therefore, worse than vain to expect to further education, especially religious education, by reducing its promoters to an unnatural uniformity of religious teaching, or to a surrender of distinctive doctrines. It would be un-English, and I think unsuccessful, to do so. At any rate, is it wise, when we are striving at a work sufficiently beset with its peculiar difficulties, to embark in a scheme which thwarts a national idiosyncracy, which, so far from opposing our efforts, powerfully aids them. Denominational zeal in the education of the poor is one of the most effective means whereby it is furthered; and, so far from being an evil, a little rivalry among their richer neighbours not unfrequently educates all the poor children in a place where assuredly mere benevolence would fail in any such result.

Now the system of aiding each religious body to educate its own children enlists this powerful agency in direct aid of the real object in view, namely, that of a sound and useful education, first and foremost in the great principles of the Christian religion, and, next, in all useful secular knowledge. And if this be achieved, albeit partly through the instrumentality of Dissent, good men, who have higher interests at heart, will not repine because good has been thus accomplished. Neither will it greatly alloy their satisfaction eventually to discover, that the sectarian element had been swamped in the substantial work of the school; and that the young minds of the scholars had but superficially learned the dogmas of theology, whilst the great truths of religion, and the principles of our common faith, were alone implanted in the heart, and permanently impressed on the memory.

It is objected, with more of subtle logic than knowledge of the actual working of the present system, that inasmuch as it renders aid incident to the religious rather than the civil character of education, and that grants are given to every religious denomination, we are bestowing them in aid of every religious tenet which may choose to seek furtherance through schools to which a modicum of secular instruction is added, thus wronging conscience, and invading religious liberty. Now, in the first place, the requirement as regards religious teaching is, we believe, simply that of reading the Bible daily, and not mentioning the tests of each sect. This clearly does not involve, or even imply, a requirement as to doctrinal teaching. That it may be, nevertheless, given, is probable; nay, that the grants so obtained may empower sectarian activities, and promote schism, is possible. It is difficult to say what human power may not be abused. The only thing, however, that can give this fear force, is its realization in practice. The system of grants has subsisted many years, and they have amounted to a considerable number, yet who, practically acquainted with the country, or any part of it, can substantiate its schismatical effect, to an extent of the least importance? Can a new sect, or even a single schism, be pointed out which owes its existence, or even its vigour, to a grant to a school? If not, even on that ground may we not appease our qualms, and say 'be at rest' to legislation? It is not very easy to proselytize children, or to make schools instruments of schism. Nor is this all. It is very well to say broadly, that the Council gives grants to all religious denominations, and therefore encourages all; but there are two items in the matter left out of view—namely, number and opinion. The grant is not given to any denomination unless the number of its children (*i.e.* its members) justifies a school. If this number does exist, it is an evidence that opinion in that locality is strong in favour of the denomination. I am not aware that a much safer standard than this can be devised, of the justice as well as expediency of such a denominational claim; or could be adopted, even if the public or the rate-payers (who, by the way, are not the public) were to regulate education, and stand banker to themselves. The abuses feared are just as much under the preventive influence of public opinion as any other abuses; and inasmuch as every additional school enhances the wholesome power of public opinion, we have in it a sufficient security against the danger our alarmists have conjured up. This check is, be it remembered, infinitely more powerful over the distribution of grants by a responsible public office, than it could ever be over the local distributors of local funds to their own neighbours. I apprehend that the largesses to sects would be greatly increased were there neither national funds, nor national responsibility in their appropriation. It seems to escape the notice of the objectors, that the same money-aid to seceders would be just as effectual to their purpose whether it came from rates or grants. True it is that, under the cogent conditions I have named, school grants are made to all denominations indifferently that come in the name of religion. We have, however, this comfort, that none who do *not* come in that name can receive it. If it be that the present system is guilty of sometimes aiding schism, it is perhaps no inadequate atonement, in the eyes of Christians, that it excludes the chance of furthering irreligion, or endowing scepticism.

It has, indeed, been strongly recommended, by men whose enlarged views and signal philanthropy entitle their suggestions to careful attention, that a school-rate by means of local assessment should be thus substituted for grants by the Committee of Council; and, as a necessary concomitant, that there should be local boards for its administration.

Now, in the first place, it may well be that the system of local and municipal government, as far as it has gone, and confined as it has been to fiscal objects, has worked tolerably well; and yet, that such power cannot be extended with like success to the administration of schools. If it be argued that it is merely proposed to confine the local boards to raising the money, without any control over its application, it is very little likely that they will assent to be thus used as mere instruments for their own taxation: if, on the contrary, it is intended that they should be invested with any such control, it is no less certain that they are not qualified to use, and ought not to have it. The usual reasons why the exercise of new powers by the central authority in the state is watched with jealous scrutiny, and ceded with reluctance, do not apply to an enlargement by them of the means of education, inasmuch as the object of the power in this case is to benefit the poor, and not those who can confer services, or repay favours. An abuse of power in the increase of popular education is a practical contradiction, for the intelligence of a people is the best security of freedom and preventive of misgovernment.

If a school-rate is adopted, with a view to give a fixed fee to the school for each child educated there, as an inducement to the parents to send their children—in the first place, such persons would rarely be payers of the rate, who must be of a class generally above those who would alone avail themselves of eleemosynary education. In the next place, the poor who did so would thereby be inured to a habit of dependence on others for the fulfilment of one of the highest duties they owe to themselves and their children. I found, even among the poor hand-loom weavers of Scotland, an universal repugnance to what they deemed the humiliation of gratuitous education. A stern necessity should alone induce us to disregard the advantages of cherishing this feeling. As far as station and self-respect are contingent on independence, the difference is not very perceptible between the recipient of education paid for by the rates, and the out-door pauper. The practical difficulty and cost of checking the payments, and apportioning them to the constantly-fluctuating attendance in schools for the poor all over the kingdom, is a minor disadvantage, though still a considerable one. If the object be merely to meet the necessities of the indigent classes in the poorer districts, it is very easy to do so, under the existing system, by giving a discretion as to the amount of grants, rendering it a condition of the grant of salary, that all or a great number of children selected by each school committee be admitted and instructed at small or merely nominal school fees. There are other means of inducing the poor to avail themselves of such privileges.

A local rate is objectionable because it is local, and therefore partial in its incidence. A wealthy district would be taxed less than a poor one, notwithstanding, as would often happen, the latter required more school aid. The burden of the rate would necessarily fall heavier on the country than on towns. In addition to these drawbacks, be it remembered that any local rate is levied only on persons who are land or householders; that is to say, a very large part of the community do not pay it at all. On what ground is this large portion to be exempted? What is there in the nature of the duty of aiding the education of the poor, which renders it incumbent only on persons who have land or houses? Why are fundholders, ship-owners, annuitants, salaried officers, clerks, shopmen, nay, even independent artisans and labour

ers, to be exempted from that duty in the same proportion
to their income ?   And why are nearly all women to be also
included in the same category?   Surely each and all of these
are just as deeply interested in the moral welfare of the people !
But how, it may be asked, is such a distribution of the incidence to be effected ?   By just leaving it as it now is.   So
long as it comes from the general revenue of the country, it
is paid by the whole community, all of whom are directly
or indirectly taxed ; and such, surely, is the most equitable
manner of levying the fund for the discharge of a national
duty.

It must also be remembered, that to levy a school-rate
at all is to add another to the existing local burdens, and
to risk unpopularity; whilst to take the same or more
money from a surplus revenue imposes no new tax, and
escapes a formidable prejudice.   If it be desirable to enlist
public sympathy in an enterprise, which can scarcely be
successful unless it be popular, this is surely a consideration
which it were an imprudence to underrate, and temerity to
disregard.

There are also some ministerial difficulties in the assessment and due appropriation of local school-rates, easily
appreciated by those who are conversant with parochial
administration, and also with the jealousies and jobbing
which often engender malversation among bodies less
likely to be beset with them than those to whom the
assessment of school-rates would be entrusted.

Assuming, however, that it were possible to escape the
operation of all these evils, and to render local boards mere
collectors of money, the above-named evil is necessarily
encountered; and, what is of still more moment, the operation of the voluntary principle, so feeble by itself, but so
valuable as an auxiliary, is excluded.

Before we launch forth on so entire a change of the
existing system, may it not be wise to consider whether its
shortcomings are really inseparable from its continuance.

Great changes are usually great evils—and a modification is preferable to the destruction of a system already in operation, with at least some measure of admitted usefulness. May it not perchance be, that the evil is in the present *scale*, rather than in the *system* of grants. To compel municipal or any local support of schools, seems to be justifiable only if all other means have been found to fail. This cannot be, unless they have been fairly tried. Now a scale of grants which gives aid on terms which are unavailable wherever aid is most needed, cannot be deemed a fair trial. Yet the present cast-iron scale inflexibly exacts, that the parish or district shall subscribe a large part of the whole sum required. But poor parishes cannot do this; and thus they who often need schools the most, and are least able to support them, are those whom the present scale leaves unaided and uneducated. Increase the annual Parliamentary grant so as to deal very liberally with such necessities. Let the Committee of Council—whose general management has inspired ample and well-deserved confidence—exercise a discretion in the aid given to each case, according to its wants, proportioning the largeness of the grant rather to the poverty of the parish than to its means of contribution; and the present system will then, and not till then, be fairly tried. There are many parishes where two-thirds, or three-fourths, of the whole amount required should be granted, whether in the shape of building grants, or in part or entire payment* of teachers' salaries.†

* It is very questionable whether it is advisable to call or treat this latter kind of aid as 'augmentations.' Why in all cases, having ascertained, by the usual examination, the standard of the teacher, and assigned his certificate, may not the grant be a *part payment* of the salary attached to it? The salary paid to each ought to be apportioned to his competency and work. To give him an augmentation, implies that his salary falls short of what it ought to be, and the augmentation assumes the untoward character of a make-weight.

† The means of testing the poverty of each district are afforded by the

Thus beneficially to enlarge the application of the aid given by the State to education, on the present well-organized, perfectly understood, and accepted system, would, I firmly believe, meet with the general assent of the country; nor is there much reason to doubt that Parliament would devote half a million of redundant revenue to that object; nor is it unlikely that such a grant might be afterwards increased. It is obviously premature to denounce the present system as inadequate, until its scope be sufficiently enlarged to enable it to do its work. It is also probable that the present semi-dormant zeal in the establishment of schools would be stimulated to activity by such new promise of success; and that apathy would disappear with the hopelessness of effort. Many a clergyman and minister are discouraged and passive, simply because they are certain of the inability of their parish or people to comply with the existing conditions of a grant. Moreover, the very increase of schools, and the spread of education, engender the desire for them, and provoke emulation. Parish *A*, well countenanced in its effortless darkness, and its non-schooled poor, by the like condition of its neighbours, is less satisfied with ignorance when parishes *B* and *C* have begun to be educated; and thus the example spreads, together with the facilities for adopting it.

But the great recommendation of a change which shall be merely fiscal is, that we shall thereby avoid the re-opening of those very mischievous feuds and contests which it has taken ten years to appease, and whose extinction has

---

rateable value of property and the amount of population and poor-rate, consideration being had of other local circumstances, which might affect either the need of schooling, or the means of supplying it by voluntary contribution. It is one of the benefits of a corps of inspectors above the suspicion of biassed judgments, that such local data can be readily and inexpensively ascertained.

been with so much difficulty achieved by the operation of
the discreet and just system which it is now—in the
first years of its success—proposed to pull down, and
replace by an untried project, which has already evoked
the opposition of Roman-catholics, and will, in all proba-
bility, create a struggle of sects, wherever their partisans
exist in the local bodies who are causelessly invited to tax
themselves for that for which the revenue already suffices,
and to meddle in a matter which its present managers
are tenfold better qualified to deal with.

There are, perhaps, fewer stronger reasons for retaining
the present system than the fact of its well-tested practicability.   This is a vast item in the success of any system, in
this country and in these times.   Nor is there a surer mode
of wasting good effort, and perilling the best causes, than to
disregard the prestige of the practical, and our idolatry of
usage, and to experimentalize in new systems, where no necessity exists of discarding those which are established. That
clamour which almost necessarily assails every infant measure affecting great interests, and at one time 'wagged its
tongue' lustily against the Committee of Council and its
grants, has now died away, or lives only in the faint
murmurs of two powerless extremes in Church and
Dissent.

The present system, at length well understood—a matter
of some ten years to accomplish—is beginning to come into
its intended operation. To increase its grants, and extend the
liberality and scale of its aid, is merely to give fuller effect
to its established design under its present organization.   It
is to sail with the stream, in unison with public feeling, and,
in fact, in compliance with a general desire.   On the other
hand, the disruptions of this system begin *de novo;* and to
establish on its ruins another scheme, which, whatever may
be its theoretical merits, will necessarily have to struggle for
years against misapprehension and hostility, and ensure pre-

judice where popularity is essential to success, is certainly likely to retard, if not to endanger, the progress of education.

The present condition and character of our schools for the poor are certainly far from fulfilling every requirement. But are their defects anywise contingent on the principle of parliamentary grants? Crippled, and stinted of sufficient means to render them effective to their purpose, many schools undeniably are; but is that a reason for anything beyond an increase of means? How can it in any way bespeak the need of another mode of raising or administering the required funds?

If, indeed, Parliament had shown a reluctance to vote adequate sums for such a purpose, that might, perhaps, have been a reason for desiring some easier and surer mode of obtaining the money; or if malversation of the present grants had taken place, and unfairness were attributed to the Committee of Council in assigning them, that indeed would be cause for the gravest dissatisfaction with a system open to such abuses; but when the fact is, that the only reluctance Parliament has ever shown has been in voting so small a sum,* whilst no *bonâ fide* suspicion has ever attached to the honour or fair dealing of the Committee of Council,† one naturally looks for some very strong reason for the proposed change—which assuredly none of its proposers have yet presented. Its administration is, in fact, becoming popular, in the widest sense of the term. So far from being regarded as an interference with individual liberty, its present system was strongly upheld by the Working Men's Association,

---

* See Mr. Henley's speech on the vote of £20,000 for parochial union schools in 1851.

† Save, perhaps, the attack of the extreme party who met at Willis's Rooms in June, 1850, and of whose misstatements its former allies seem heartily to repent.

even when democratic tendencies were far rifer than now. In its *Address to the Working Classes on National Education,** after having dilated on the benefits of education, it says :—

But how, it may be asked, are the means to be provided? We may reply by asking, how were the means provided for less worthy purposes? We remember that twenty millions were paid to compensate the owners of slaves for relinquishing their unjust traffic. That the means were provided for paying extravagant pensions, and for erecting useless palaces to royalty, and are still found to support an almost interminable list of idlers from year to year. Whence, too, we may inquire, came our means to war against freedom wherever it raised its head, and to assist all the despots of Europe to keep their people in ignorance and slavery? Were but half the anxiety evinced to train the human race in peace and happiness, as has hitherto been exerted to keep them in subjection to a few despots, abundant means would be afforded for the purpose.

But though we hold it to be the duty of Government to raise the means of education, by taxation or otherwise, to see it properly apportioned, in the erecting of suitable and sufficient schools, and for superintending them so far as to see the original intention of the people carried into effect, we are decidedly opposed to the placing such immense power and influence in the hands of Government as that of selecting the teachers and superintendents, the books and kinds of instruction, and the whole management of schools in each locality. While we want a uniform and just system of education, we must guard against the influence of irresponsible power and public corruption; we are opposed, therefore, to all concentration of power beyond that which is absolutely necessary to make and execute the laws ; for, independent of its liability to be corrupt, it destroys those local energies, experiments, and improvements, so desirable to be fostered for the advancement of knowledge, and prostrates the whole nation before one uniform despotism.

It would be difficult more accurately to describe the exact extent to which the Government does, by the existing system, raise the means of education, properly apportion it, and superintend schools, without interfering so far

---

* It is signed, among others, by Henry Vincent, Henry Hetherington, and William Lovett.

as to select teachers, books, or to undertake their management, leaving local energies in full and unlimited operation.

The higher and middle classes, including the clergy, have given ample proof of their approval of this mode of aiding schools, by largely availing themselves of grants, and desiring more. In fine, it is difficult to understand the ground on which the substitution of local rating for a system so highly sanctioned as the existing one, is proposed ; and assuredly no adequate one is stated by its proposers.

The first need is that of increased grants.

CHAPTER II.

Need of Better Schools.

THE second need is of a far more efficient system of education in our schools—an education consisting both of training and teaching. True it is, that there has been a numerical increase alike of schools and scholars of late years, and that there has been also taught a considerably higher amount of unintellectual acquirement than formerly, and a smattering of subjects which thirty years ago were not taught at all. So that if the success of schools is to be measured by the number of scholars, and the amount of education by that of reading, writing, and arithmetic, it is undeniable that we have reason to plume ourselves on our efforts, and repose on our laurels. But if we are to deal with school children as future men and women, to whose welfare our present education is the passport—welfare dependent tenfold more on those moral qualities and industrial faculties which will fit them for the duties of their station in life, than on mere scholarship, then it is to be feared that there is a certain amount of actual failure in our apparent success. It is difficult otherwise to understand such facts, for instance, as that, out of 957 convict boys admitted to Parkhurst, no less than 360 (above one-third part) had been not only nominally 'educated' in national schools, but *for considerable periods.** Perhaps this results from the defective character of the religious instruction given, and the total absence of all moral and industrial training worth the name, in a large majority of our present schools for the poor. May it not also be feared, that incomparably more time and skill are devoted to a fragmentary and imperfect secular instruction, pursued to the sacrifice of the infinitely more important work of teaching useful knowledge, and the training of mind, heart and hand? Now if this be so, the sharpening of the wits alone, and the mere collection of a number of children together, coming and going, moreover, by themselves, will have a necessary tendency to create bad habits and foster contamination. To increase the mere mechanical agencies of the mind, *without moral culture*, speaking generally, is as sure to demoralize, as it is certain that our hearts are naturally prone to evil. Now what are the evidences that such various defects exist in our present school system?

The direct evidence consists in the statements of those who are the best enabled, by opportunity, skill, and experience, to ascertain the fact, and who are not only men of irreproachable veracity, but who are necessarily unwilling witnesses to the truths they feel constrained to tell, by a sense of the duty their office imposes on them—I mean the Inspectors of Schools, and especially those of Church

---

* *Report on Prison Discipline*, p. 513.

schools. In turning to the latest of these reports,* we
find the Reverend Mr. Moseley speaking thus:—

The conception of what really belongs to elementary education is as yet very imperfectly formed in this country; and if
the present promoters of schools had abundance of funds placed
at their disposal, and were called upon to-morrow to realize
their idea of it, *I can imagine nothing more absurd than the
result.*

The Rev. Mr. Blandford says :—

The acquaintance with Scripture, and the intelligent knowledge of the catechism, which many of the upper classes in these
schools exhibit, is very pleasing; but the great defect which
characterizes the religious instruction is, that it is not sufficiently
practical, nor incorporated as it should be in the daily routine of
the school. The children learn texts of the Bible by heart, are
fairly acquainted with the outline of Scripture history, and can
prove points of doctrine ; but when questioned as to their *practical application and bearing upon our every-day life and intercourse with each other*, the inference, however obvious, can
seldom be drawn. I believe the masters of our national schools
to be, as a body, a respectable class of men ; but they are deficient in that deep religious feeling, the expression of which will
be visible in a thousand ways in the management of their schools,
and will be identified, in a greater or less degree, with the conduct of the children ; that this one thing is wanting there is the
testimony of the clergy to appeal to, who have daily and personal
intercourse with them, and who complain of the want of this all-
important element in their character.

Again : as to secular instruction, he observes that—

The little use that teachers make of the chalk and black
board, otherwise than for setting copies and giving the children
sums in arithmetic, is a significant proof how slight is their
acquaintance with teaching as an art.

The Rev. Mr. Kennedy, in his report, writes thus:—

I have endeavoured in every case, as far as time would
allow, to ascertain the amount of religious knowledge among
the children of the schools in my district. I cannot speak in
high terms of the average proficiency in this subject. Before
examining a class in arithmetic, I commonly ask the master
what rules they can work ; the answer sometimes is, 'Oh, any-

---

* *Minutes of Council for* 1850-51.

thing—decimals, interest, mensuration, &c.;' and in most cases I have found the boys unable to work with accuracy sums in simple subtraction and division.

After complaining of defective organization, Mr. Kennedy sums up his comments thus :—

So distracted, indeed, are all the elements of popular education—and, if I am not travelling too far out of my sphere, I would add, so distracted are they in all departments of education, from national schools to the great public schools, and from training schools to the universities—that I feel as if nothing thoroughly systematic and effective, nothing worthy of the sums expended, and worthy of this great nation, would be accomplished, till the whole business of education be methodically organized and adjusted, under the responsible care of a Minister and Board of Public Instruction. At present there is an immense waste of force. The energy which is exerted, the money which is expended, is almost like the work of the Danaïdes or of Ixion, so wasted is it all, or so counteracted.

The Rev. Mr. Norris observes—

That in order to cram a more than heretofore amount of acquirement into a shorter than heretofore period of schooling, several of our teachers are sacrificing in a great measure all that makes education truly valuable to men as citizens and as Christians. And I am constrained to add, that this is precisely the impression left upon my mind by more than one-third of the higher order of schools that I have visited.

As to industrial training, nearly all the inspectors report that it has scarcely an existence.

The Rev. Mr. Watkins finds an improvement in the quality of the education given, but portrays an evil which defeats its effect, in the very early age at which the children leave school :

One might (he says) almost state it thus :—that *about five children out of* 100 *of the poorer classes stay at school to an age when they may learn something, and when their characters may be moulded into shape.* Is not this a mockery of education?

In every report (he afterwards adds) it has been my duty to notice the tender age of the children in elementary schools, the gradual lowering of that age in the great majority of those places, and the contemporaneous shortening of the school-time of the children. This evil has now, I conceive, grown to such magnitude, that it *must* be remedied. All the partial restoratives have failed to touch this disease. All the roundabout methods of treatment have not reached its source. Its cause still remains :

Tolle mali causam, tollitur omne malum.

But can this be done? What is its cause? The value of the child's work in the market, either of manufacturing or agricultural labour, and the want of its wages at home.

This is no doubt the cause, and its existence proves and points most clearly to the deficiency in useful and practical training which exists in our school system. In a word, the parents do not value the schooling the children get, simply because it is not valuable. Make it so, and the remedy will be attained.

The poor are not bad judges of the value of what they purchase—poverty makes them so; and although it is not in the nature of things that ignorance should rightly appreciate knowledge, it is not difficult so to adapt the knowledge we give poor children to their wants, as to make its value felt by the dullest parent. It is because we do not so adapt it, that the parents do not feel the benefits of education. It is our fault, not theirs. Their child comes home coated with crude learning, which they cannot understand, and perhaps do not much undervalue in thinking it worthless. But this they *do* understand—that their child is none the better fitted for work, and all the less inclined to it; that his learning has not improved his love for them, or school discipline his obedience; that Scripture lessons have not made him religious, nor catechisms moral; and albeit he can entangle himself in tare and tret, trace the Nile, and name the prophets, greater and less, wiser people than his parents are prone to estimate such attainments as dearly purchased, at the sacrifice of homelier virtues and handier faculties; and the notion runs strongly and spreads widely, among many a class above the peasants, that *we are over-educating our poor*—filling their heads and puffing them up with comparatively useless knowledge. Perhaps it is not *useless;* but can we honestly say it is as *useful* as we are capable of making it? Most certainly not—it were the worst kind of pedantry to say so.

The false estimates of our progress arise in various ways. First, as to the efficiency of the schools. The faults under which they usually labour are these: they are either entirely and obviously incapable of teaching at all, or they present certain appearances of efficiency which are more or less deceptive. There is another class of schools, which teaches the ordinary acquirements efficiently, and yet fails to give the children moral or industrial training. Of the first class, nothing need be said. Of those which present deceptive appearances of teaching well, the number has probably much increased with the growing interest taken in education, and with the concern the teachers have in creating a good impression of their success.

The devices for passing off a bad school, so as to make it appear a good one at an examination, are manifold, and many teachers study them as an art. I have known old scholars who had left, and even children who never belonged to the school at all, introduced into the first class on such occasions; but the most common device is, to cram the first class with rote answers to previously-prepared questions. This is an exceedingly convenient and successful plan; for, inasmuch as the questions are so selected that the bystanders could not answer them themselves, not only are they astounded at the children's proficiency, but entirely deterred from adventuring on any examination on their own account. At an annual display of the kind at a school in Shropshire, the master objects to any other questioning than his own—'it puts the children out!' At another, where the tributaries of the Mississippi were correctly enumerated to the master, and the geographical attainments were passing off with great *éclat*, a pertinacious visitor persisted in a few home inquiries about English rivers, and found the whole class utterly unconscious of the existence of the Mersey.   But in nineteen cases out of twenty the fraud passes undiscovered.   The best way to break it down is for all visitors, however humble their own sphere of attainments, to persist in getting answers to plain questions on simple subjects which are within it.   It either supports the genuineness of the display in the higher flights, or it breaks it down and exposes it on the spot. In arithmetic, it is no uncommon trick to cram the children in particular sums, which the master sets: or where the class can work them they are written down for them, and thus numeration is not tested; in the lower classes, it is always essential to dictate *vivâ voce* a compound addition sum which shall test this elementary branch; it is frequently neglected, and children can cast fairly, who have no notion how to numerate and write down money-sums correctly.

Mr. Tufnell, one of H. M. Inspectors of Union Schools, says in his last report :—

The longer experience I have as a School Inspector, the more impressed I am with the necessity of exercising extreme caution before pronouncing on the character of the instruction given in any school.   Under some circumstances, I believe it almost impossible to discover what the children know.   An examination, before a large and promiscuous assembly, appears to me the most inexpedient of all methods of testing what has been taught.   The children are required to play their parts in a public spectacle, and I should no more expect them to do so without particular and special preparation, than I should expect a drama to be well performed on the stage without previous rehearsal.   To put really searching questions to children placed in so novel a position is unfair; and though in a first-rate school, much accustomed to be examined by strangers, the children may pass such an ordeal with credit, in nine-tenths of schools what is really known cannot be elicited by such a proceeding. Accordingly, I believe it not an uncommon practice, in public exhibitions of schools, to settle beforehand everything that is to be asked or answered.   This plan sometimes leads to untimely

replies. In one meeting of this description, the master inter-
rupted the boys while reading the Scriptures with a question
intended to show their ready knowledge of the Bible, thus :
' Now, children, perhaps you will be able to refer to that beautiful passage in'—before he could proceed any further, all the
class shouted out the passage required. But mental arithmetic
offers the most convenient field for making a favourable impression on a public audience. Children may easily be taught
the extended multiplication-table, and this alone is sufficient to
startle many persons unacquainted with the subject, and who
are unaware of the arithmetical tricks by which many apparently
very difficult questions are solved by a simple and easy effort of
memory. I once threw a teacher into confusion—who was
asking such questions as ' What are 18 times 45 ?' and getting
instantaneous answers—by asking how many half-crowns there
were in a pound, which proved too difficult for them.

The most frequent defect is in this practical application
of the rules. There are many school teachers well versed
in the higher rules who never teach how to apply the lower
ones; and multitudes of scholars who work long-division,
and sometimes even reduction of money and practice, sums,
fail utterly in the simplest kind of mental arithmetic. How
much will four ounces of tea cost at 5s. per lb. ? and what is
five feet of lace at 9s. per yard? will often floor a whole
school, in which the arithmetic, as displayed by the teacher,
has gone off famously. In the most important of all
branches of instruction—religious knowledge—the defects
are, in all tolerably good schools, less easily detected. Shy-
ness is oftener a genuine plea in this than in any other
branch of instruction. It is often, however, most shamefully
neglected. The rote system comes generally in aid of the
master. The catechism is a great make-weight. Five
people out of six who examine, or hear an examination in
it, are satisfied with the rote answers; and nineteen out of
twenty are delighted if the children can pass muster in the
broken catechism, which is no more than a second edition
of answers by rote. Of course the *actual* amount that the
child comprehends is nowise tested, and in most cases,

where questioning proceeds no further, they comprehend next to nothing. It is a very common dodge to instruct two or three children who answer well, and so hide the ignorance of the rest.

Frequently, where a portion of the Holy Scriptures has been read, and the questioning takes place on it, it is in such a manner that the questions are suggested by the answers as they are read in the book, or at most repeated from the memory only. The child reads, for example—' Peter went up into the housetop to pray.' *'Who went up?'*—'Peter.' *'Where did he go?'*—'Into the housetop.' *'What for?'* —'To pray.' This is done sometimes with the book open and sometimes shut; in either case, it is no effort of the mind, nor is the child made to think. It is only when the questions require thought in order to be answered, that the real value of the instruction is ascertained. Many a school passes muster until it is examined to some better effect, and it is then found that no answer can be obtained to questions such as these:—What duty are we reminded of in the Lord's Prayer by the words, ' Forgive us our trespasses as we forgive them that trespass against us ?' Which commandment are we put in mind of by the words ' Hallowed be Thy name ?' Which parables teach us the duty of prayer—of repentance—of the good use of our faculties ? How does the parable of the good Samaritan teach us to do good to our enemies ? What do the words ' There is no health in us,' in the confession of sins, mean ? what great truth does it convey ? Which of the words, in our duty towards God in the catechism, mean that we ought to pray to him ? If you tell tales of another child, which commandment do you break ? Mention any of the types of Christ, and name the points of resemblance. How does our Lord's death save us ? What must we do to profit by it ? What are we taught is the fulfilling of the law, and by what parables and precepts did our Lord enforce it ? Any questions which require thought to answer, and which relate to any great duty or principle, such as ought to be plainly impressed on the child's mind, will thus fairly test the school and its teacher. A similar mode of questioning should be applied in each branch of the education given. Any examination short of this is worthless ; and a school which will not pass successfully under such an ordeal is scarcely worthy of the name of a school. Still less easily will it pass successfully if the children are examined in useful knowledge. Only in the higher order of schools is this taught at all.

The dean of Hereford (Mr. Dawes) has, in his admirable *Hints on Secular Education,* familiarized the public with the mode in which this may be readily done in the school-room; and in the following pages it is designed to show how it may be further developed and practised in industrial employment. If the object of instruction be to render the child more able to fulfil the duties of his station in life, as well physical as moral, it is surely evident that, at any rate, useful knowledge, relating, for example, to the arts of life, is of the first utility. According to the old notion and practice of schools, it is undeniable that no such instruction had a place. But the question is, whether the new requirements and circumstances of these times do not render an education for the working classes exceedingly defective which omits it. When we perceive the ease and success with which such instruction may be given, and how practicable it is, the reasonableness of classing it among the requirements of good schools will appear less questionable. On the expediency, however, of imparting a practical knowledge of the arts of life, which can be given without the accessories—in some cases impossible—for industrial training, no question is admissible. Let schools be tested by the amount of useful knowledge of all kinds which they teach children—not merely to repeat from memory, but to understand and to apply. If this be done faithfully, a very moderate estimate of their actual value will result.

Another false estimate of the progress of education relates to the existing amount of education, which has been much exaggerated. In 1847, Mr. Edward Baines, of Leeds, addressed some letters to Lord John Russell, in which he endeavoured to prove a large and gratifying increase of scholars. Dr. Hook, of Leeds, has also made some erroneous estimates of their increase. I have given in the appendix (A) some evidence of the untrustworthiness of their statistics, and the entire fallacy of conclusions built on such data. Since then, the grants made by the Committee of Council indicate tolerably the increase which has taken place; for so general has been the desire to avail themselves of grants, that few promoters of schools for the poor have foregone their aid. The grants, therefore, indicate nearly the increased number of schools; and it is as follows:—

In the Minutes for 1849-50 there is a detailed statement of all the grants made for the 'erection, enlargement, and *improved fittings,*' of all schools aided by grants from 1833 to October 31st, 1849, a period of sixteen years, during which the following is an abstract of the whole:—

	Total Grants.	Number of Schools aided in any way.	Number of Scholars.		Number of Schools in which the average is taken.
			Daily average attendance.	Number accommodated.	
	£				
England . .	399,358	3255	246,979	539,202	2171
Wales . . .	27,418	198	12,540	24,579	121
Scotland . .	41,563	302	24,065	39,230	205
Total . .	468,339	3755	283,584	603,011	2497

Assuming that the proportion of attendance to schools here given applies to the whole of the 3755 schools, then 426,454 children actually attend them.

A portion of these grants, and also of the 603,011 children accommodated, and of the 426,454 daily attendance of children, belong to schools which were in existence before 1833, and which figure in this list merely as having been aided in respect of fittings and enlargements, &c. Without making any deduction in respect of these, and crediting the whole number of the daily attendance as a net increase of scholars during the sixteen years, to what does this 426,454 amount ?· Why, to less than the actual increase of the juvenile population in the same time who are within the scope of the schools in question, namely, one-eighth of the whole increase.* It may be urged, that many schools have been established or enlarged without the aid of grants during this period. But it may be doubted whether they do not form a small portion of the whole, and may be fairly set off against the scholars and schools before in existence, and included in the above table.

The undeniable effect of true education on morals has been too largely credited to the past and present schools, and the laudable endeavour to vindicate the principle has led some good men into a false estimate of the practical effect of a shallow schooling, which, in reality, neither embodies the principle of education nor produces its fruits.

The statistics of crime and schooling have been unintentionally perverted to the support of this mistake. The most careful use of the only available statistics of crime and education is necessarily imperfect, and it must be premised that so are the deductions drawn from them. As far, however, as they enable us to judge, they show that such schooling as our humbler classes have hitherto had leads rather to crime than to virtue. There are, of course, many, and, happily, increasing exceptions to this rule among the really

---

* The total increase of population in Great Britain, from 1833 to 1850, was about 3,657,000.

good schools which the recent progress in education produces; but, as regards the class old enough to have already come under the penalties of the law, as a general rule the most ignorant and unschooled are not the most criminal— the most criminal having been those whose instruction shows them, at any rate, to have had some schooling.

The amount of instruction possessed by criminal offenders is ascertained at the gaols, and used to be given in each annual report of the Home Office; it resulted thus from 1838 to 1847:—

Degrees of Instruction.	Mean of 1838—1842.	Mean of 1843—1847.	Difference.
Unable to read and write . . .	33·36	30·68	2·68
Able to read and write imperfectly	55·49	58·72	3·23
Able to read and write well . .	8·46	8·00	0·46
Instruction superior to reading and writing well . . .	0·34	0·37	0·03
Instruction could not be ascertained	2·34	2·21	0·13

Thus, out of the above number of criminals, amounting to 228,806, during the above period, from 1838 to 1847 inclusive, no less than $65\frac{1}{2}$ per cent. were schooled, and a decided minority perfectly ignorant; and this disproportion, so far from being diminished by fresh schools for the poor, has been on the increase together with crime itself. Neither can the disproportion be explained by an assumption, that the schooled or instructed portion of the people largely exceeds that of the ignorant, and thus accounts for the disproportion; for the fact is otherwise. The National School Association took great pains to ascertain this so recently as 1850; and, notwithstanding a large increase of schools, they state in their address, dated May, 1850, ' nearly one-half of this great nation is unable to read and write.' Now, if we deduct from the half who *are* able all

the upper classes, and those who are not within the temptation of crime, it must be that, of the classes out of which
nearly all crime springs, a large majority are ignorant.
Hence the fact, that nevertheless so large a per-centage as
65 of the criminals are more or less instructed, tends to
prove very strongly, that the sort of instruction possessed
by them, and by the lower classes generally, promotes instead
of preventing crime. Assuming that in the following para-
graphs the National School Association, by the words ' untaught' and ' not educated,' mean not properly educated,
they contain some truth, and draw from practical experience
a fearful picture:—

The existing means for popular education is, for the most
part, poor in quality, as well as insufficient in amount.

Our gaols and our poor-houses are full. Our cities, our
towns, and our villages contain, in a large proportion of their
inhabitants, persons who are vicious, criminal, or destitute,
because they are untaught. The ranks of this large class are
constantly recruited from the great numbers of young persons
of both sexes for whom no educational provision exists; for
while the population is rapidly increasing, little comparatively is
doing for the extension or the improvement of education.

Such is the state in which the country has been left by those
in whose hands has been the care of popular education. These
parties may be classed under two heads:—1, the Established
Church; 2, the Dissenters. The Established Church of this
kingdom is the most opulent and the most powerful corporation
in the world. It claims the right to educate the people, but for
the most part has neglected the duty, for the people are not
educated. The Dissenters have, by their voluntary efforts,
effected something for the education of the people. The joint
operations of the Established Church and the Dissenters have
proved insufficient, for the people are not educated; the joint
operations of the Established Church and the Dissenters have
left us with a small modicum of intelligence, a preponderating
mass of ignorance, crime, pauperism, and wretchedness. Something else is necessary.

And that something is a practically religious, moral, and
industrial training. But ere we open the more practical
pages of this little book, let us examine another of the

theoretical mistakes we are desirous of putting out of our way. It has been found that the local statistics of crime, compared in gross with the returns of education gathered from the number of those who sign their names in the marriage registers, in each corresponding county, show a similar concurrence between criminality and so-called instruction. Now these marriage-register marks are certainly not a reliable index of education ; but it is the opinion of certain able statisticians, that they afford the best approximation to it which we possess, the census returns of schools not being yet published. In appendix (B) will therefore be found a table giving the population—the persons to each hundred acres—total criminal offences, divided into grave and minor, for the three years, 1848, '49, and '50, and the per-centage of both sexes who signed the marriage-register with marks in 1848. The result of this table is, that selecting the ten most instructed counties and the ten least instructed, including South and North Wales, the most instructed are the most criminal, both as to grave and minor crimes, as will be seen from the following short table :—

Ten *most* instructed Counties.	Persons signing Marriage Registers with Marks.	Grave Crimes in every 1000 Persons.	Minor Crimes in every 1000 Persons.	Ten *least* instructed Counties.	Persons signing Marriage Registers with Marks.	Grave Crimes in every 1000 Persons.	Minor Crimes in every 1000 Persons.
Westmld.	17·2	·34	2·63	Kent	56·8	·73	4·04
Cumberld.	23·3	·32	1·90	Monmth.	56·5	·99	5·21
Northumb	29·1	·57	1·87	S. Wales	55·2	·43	2·38
Rutland	29·8	·94	3·74	N. Wales	55·0	·45	1·98
Sussex . .	31·1	·59	3·90	Bedford .	52·6	·65	3·40
Devon . .	31·7	·48	4·10	Stafford .	51·6	·72	4·32
Middlesex	33·0	·85	5·70	Herts	50·6	·82	4·81
Gloucester	33·2	·85	6.35	Lancash.	50·3	·69	4·34
Derby. .	35·9	·44	2·48	Bucks	49·2	·95	4·88
Oxon . .	36·1	·61	4·38	Salop. .	48·8	·59	3·31
Total Averages	32·0	0·70	4·65	Total Averages	50·6	0·67	3·88

It had, previously to the publication of the returns for these later years, been said, by an able writer on the subject, that a vagrant class, bred in the districts where the grave crimes abound, migrate from thence into the more instructed districts, where the *minor* crimes abound, which the said class therefore commit, rather than the native population of such districts. That people bred in districts prone to the graver crimes should, on migrating to other districts, instead of swelling the catalogue of such crimes, swell only the amount of minor crimes, requires support; and certainly derives none from the mere fact, that in the best instructed and most populous districts the minor, rather than the major offences prevail. It never was, however, by any means evident that the grave class of offences are less committed by vagrants than others, or that the minor ones, such as larceny, are more generally committed by them. And it is now proved that the entire theory is erroneous; and that these statistics concur with the foregoing, and indicate the brotherhood of faulty schooling and greater criminality of all kinds.

There are many other proofs of the same effect. Of 957 convicts sent to Parkhurst, independently of those who had had some smattering of instruction, no less than 360 had been educated in national schools, and most of them for a long period. Many such instances can be cited. Truly does the Rev. Benjamin Parsons, in his able work, entitled *Education the Birthright of every Human Being,* after doing ample justice to the good which day-schools have effected, proceed thus to comment on their short-comings :—

Suffice it to say, that little comparatively has yet been effected. Myriads of our race who pass for persons of education have not yet learnt what intellectual and moral powers they possess ; how to govern themselves and perfect their characters ; what is their chief business upon earth ; and what the reckoning that awaits them at the Divine tribunal. What they ought to be, and what they can be, on earth, and what they must be in eternity, seem to have hardly occupied a thought.

The schools of the higher classes of society have, in thousands of instances, been undeserving the name. The schools of the middle classes have been nearly as bad ; *and the schools for the working portion of the people have too often been nothing better than a mockery.*

They have too often been 'nothing better than a mockery,' —a mockery, moreover, of the most mischievous description, for they have left one-half of the people in profound ignorance, and have frequently aided the natural powers of evil in the rest. The wretchedly-superficial instruction we used to give in reading and writing, and the other mechanical rudiments of learning, *if alone imparted,* often result in crime. Can facts speak more plainly than these ? We have given the form of instruction, without its life and spirit. We have created instruments, without teaching how to use them, and of which the proneness of human nature to evil renders the abuse all but inevitable. Our ' education' has been no education: it has taught the alphabet of abilities without the capacity to turn them to good account. It has done too little to inform the mind or improve the disposition, but enough to feed pride and empower passion. Scanty, indeed, has been that higher knowledge which teaches a man to know himself, and opens, by mental culture, the fruitfulness of knowledge, and those rich stores of information which that culture imparts desire to retain and power to profit by. The natural offspring of our past system is to be found in the growth of selfish principles, cold hearts, and froward will. Is this safe ? is it politic ? is it prudent ? Will it give more development to weal or to woe ? Will it create for us a people who live for time, or for eternity ? Will it rear men governed by moral influence—mindful of the golden rule—good citizens, and good Christians—or will it create so much lawless energy, swinging to and fro in society, dependent on accident for its working; arm evil propensities; misapply talent; intrust clever heads and corrupt hearts to strong hands, and sow broadcast the seeds of moral debility and crime throughout the land? Schools form men, and men the times: look at the fruits before us. Was there ever a period when mental opportunities were so abundant, and mental powers so insignificant? Has there often been a greater dearth of high purpose and generous impulse? or a time when men looked more keenly to their own interests, and more coldly on the common weal? Philanthropy and patriotism, indeed, nobly strive in their generation; but how sorely thwarted by the dominant indifference to principle, and idolatry of profit, which characterize the times, and wither many of the best enterprises of our best men.

We live in days perilous to principle, and some think even to our national welfare; and need may come to muster all that is sound-hearted among the people, in defence of all that is dearest and worthiest in the institutions and liberties we possess. God forefend the danger; but should it come, as come it may, is it from the schooling we have been bestowing that we dare look with confidence for sound judgment and prompt bravery for the truth among the people, in face of all peril and all temptation? Or is there not, despite all the efforts on which we are so prone to plume ourselves, a mass of mental shallowness and moral weakness, of vanity and venality, apt for subjugation, and averse to self-sacrifice, too long neglected, amongst men on whom, in the hour of trial, we may call in vain to rally, under the banner they have never learnt to honour? In the words of Raleigh, 'may we yet gather a policy no less wise than eternal, by the comparison of other men's forepassed miseries with their own errors and ill deservings.'

CHAPTER III.

How to make Schools thoroughly useful for Poor Children.

IT should be remembered that, in dealing with the education of children, we are dealing with moral infirmities to
be cured, or diseases to be prevented, as well as with bodies
and minds to be trained and instructed. That the bulk of
our schools have as yet done neither, is sufficiently evident
to those who are able and willing (few are both) to inves-
tigate their actual condition thoroughly and dispassion-
ately. The prejudices against education, though much
reduced among the first and second classes of society,*
linger very largely among the third class; and a prevalent
indifference to it certainly exists among the fourth and fifth
classes. A small minority of society thus really cares for,
and strives to promote it.

The prejudice of the three higher classes arises from a
dislike and distrust of its effects, and the indifference of the
lower classes from a disbelief of its benefits. What with over-
teaching and under-teaching, I regard the prejudice natural,
and the indifference inevitable. Education has not been
—and what is more, it is not sufficiently—in harmony
with the position of the labouring class, for whom it is
designed; nor does it supply them with the information

---

* It is convenient thus to divide them. There is a class, evidently
above the middle class (an ambiguous term), often called the aristocracy.
Without defining it too narrowly, it may constitute the first class. Then
come the professions, the minor gentry, merchants, &c. The third class
comprises tradesmen, yeomen, farmers, &c. (once termed the *épicier* class,
from the French.) The fourth class comprises all independent labourers;
and paupers, vagabonds, prostitutes, criminals, &c., form the fifth or
dangerous class.

or skill of which they will in after-life stand especially in need.

The first objection arises naturally in the mind of those, who judge of the benefit of education by the results of what they hear called by that name.   An education radically defective in its chief elements for the most part exists in the country, and its fruits tend rather to evil than to good. Immoralities, insubordination, conceit, disinclination to hard labour and continuous industry, though they are not *necessary* results of superficial instruction, are promoted by it.   Practical experience in country districts teaches the farmer to prefer the labourer or servant who cannot write, simply because he finds that those who can, oftener wrong him than those who cannot.   From this frequent fact, he draws a wrong conclusion.   He mistakes reading and writing for education, and attributes evils to its existence which are owing to its absence.   It is difficult to convince him that it is not teaching reading and writing that does the mischief, but teaching nothing else.   Reading and writing and arithmetic, to an educated mind, are as limbs to the body, or sails to the ship; but they can effect, *if given alone*, nothing for good conduct.   They are mechanical, not moral elements.   They can no more make a good man, than a crucible can make a chemist, or a plough a ploughman.

Hence the practical operation of the system, as I have stated, not only is hurtful to the future lives of the children, but results in discredit to education.   It is believed to do more harm than good; and until we are enabled, by better systems and schools, to spread abroad among the people examples of the practical fruits of real education, so that men who thus reason may have proofs of their error before their eyes, it is almost hopeless to wrestle with it effectually.

The objection to the education of poor children on

account of its intrinsic value to them, is much the most formidable one to its progress.   Often, to convince some people of the good effects of proper education, is to confirm their hostility to its being given to the poor, for fear their children should obtain a start over their superiors.

But if the children of class three do not get their due, that fact is a strong reason for giving it to them with all possible expedition, but assuredly it is none for withholding what is also due from class four.   The instruction of the former cannot be furthered by the ignorance of the latter; on the contrary, the instruction of the poorer would be a wholesome stimulus to that of the richer.   The objection arises, unfortunately, from the narrowest and most pitiful feeling of our nature—that of selfish pride, and it deserves no quarter.   It is indispensable that, in order to make schools for the poor efficient for their purpose, we should take it for granted that they ought to be so.

The main points which will minister to this end are these:—

First,—To make the children thoroughly understand that which it is most useful for them to learn.

Secondly,—To train their morals.

Thirdly,—As far as practicable to train them in industry.

The practical means of compassing each of these objects will be treated of severally.   It may be expedient, however, to introduce them by a few general comments.

The first point needs no argument.   That which is worth doing, is worth doing well; the short-comings on this score have been already noticed, and the subjects taught are often but little better chosen.   The great fault is, that the education of the poor is seldom rudimentary enough, and too little attention is paid to the fact, that half the words used in the books they read are entirely strange to them. If these are not explained, instead of being educated the child is merely exercised in a jargon of words, which impart neither instruction nor ideas to his mind. The intense love of display which animates so many teachers, induces them to teach higher subjects, and more of them, than can benefit the child, even if he understood them.

As regards moral training, it may be conceded that it cannot be successfully given merely in the school-room.

Mr. Stow, in his exposition of the admirable system he has adopted in his Glasgow training, observes—

Moral training is, of course, practical throughout, and is the main end and object of the whole system in every department. It comprehends the restraining of all the evil propensities of our nature, and, on the contrary, a cultivation of all that is noble and virtuous, founded on Bible training; in other words, on the principles of the immutable standard of revealed truth, and stimulated by its high sanctions and motives.

We must here notice a fundamental error in education, which is the confounding of two things essentially distinct. Moral instruction and moral training are generally imagined to mean the same thing; whereas the former is merely the imparting of knowledge, and the latter is the cultivation of the practical habit. On this clear and practical distinction hangs one chief peculiarity of our system.

Habits are so important a part of education, and so influential on individuals as well as nations, that we may almost be said to be the children of habit. Proceeding, then, on this idea, how important must early training be before *habits* are formed, and when we have only evil *propensities* to contend with.

A few of the evil propensities and habits may be mentioned, which it is the duty of the trainer to restrain and suppress as they are developed; whether mental, in the school gallery, or practical, in the school play-ground, viz., rudeness, selfishness, deceit, indecency, disorder, evil speaking, cruelty, want of courtesy, anger, revenge, injustice, impatience, covetousness, and dishonesty, so fearfully general in society.

On the contrary, all the amiable feelings and christian virtues must be cultivated, such as speaking truth, obedience to parents and all in lawful authority, honesty, justice, forbearance, generosity, gentleness, kindness, fidelity to promises, courteousness, habits of attention, docility, disinterestedness, kindness to inferior animals, pity for the lame and the distressed, and the weak in intellect, and, in general, doing to others as we would wish to be done by.

Such evil propensities must be subdued, and moral habits formed, not by teaching, but by training. We cannot lecture a child into good manners, or change habits of any kind by the longest speech. The physical, intellectual, or moral habit, is only changed by a succession, or rather by a repetition of *doings*.

This department requires a *play-ground* for moral development and sympathy, as the intellectual department does a gallery for mental sympathy.

That which Mr. Stow proposes to effect by the play-ground, I would, wherever practicable, endeavour to do by industrial employment. The principle of the system would be the same, embodying the same practical working out of the rules of moral conduct, and the faculties of the moral being. In the ordinary school-room, little can be done beyond the mere teaching of ethics; this is not moral training, any more than the possession of a library is knowledge, or a sermon religion. Children especially require to be taught the application of what they learn, in order that they should profit by it. The disposition of the child, whether for good or evil, is imperfectly developed under the constraint and formality of the school-room. The play-ground, or the field, gives scope for the free working of nature—feelings, passions, and talents obtain free scope; and in this unconstrained state alone can these be ascertained, moulded, encouraged, or uprooted. Much may be done *towards* this in the school-room, and it would be very unfair to depreciate the earnest efforts, by precept and school discipline, rewards and punishments, to minister towards it in all *good* schools; but, after all, if the observation of conduct be confined to the room, the work is not, and cannot be, thoroughly accomplished. Moreover, until lately, the duty of moral training (ignored in nearly all inferior schools) has been but very scantily acknowledged or enforced in any of the very valuable works on education which its friends have published. After Mr. Stow, Mr. Dunn has probably said more on the subject than any other;

and he laments the imperfect manner in which it is carried
out. In his very able work, entitled *The Principles of
Teaching*, he remarks:—

In moral education, a twofold work has to be accomplished :
'the faculty of reason must be taught how to judge rightly
between truth and error, good and evil,' and *the habit of acting*
rightly must be formed in order that the imagination, the passions, and the affections, may be accustomed to bow to the
decisions of reason, when thus enlightened and strengthened.
The first of these (the formation of right judgments) has long
been a primary object of our efforts; the last (the formation of
habits and the regulation of emotions) has not yet received that
share of attention which its paramount importance demands. It
may be worth inquiry whether more cannot be done in this way
than has hitherto been considered practicable.

I am convinced, not only from long observation of the
existing short-comings in the ordinary schools, but by practical experience of a different system at Quatt and other
industrial schools, that efficient moral training can be
best accomplished where industrial labour out of school
is combined with religious and secular instruction in
school; and I believe horticulture and farm-work by far
the best adapted for the purpose. It seems to have these
recommendations as regards moral training: first, the child
is thereby taught to be useful, and receives perhaps his
earliest lesson in labour. This is a great step in moral
elevation, and herein does industrial employment distance
the playground, which affords no such advantage. In the
next place, the work done is of a kind to call into operation
not only more of the faculties of mind and body, but also
of the moral feelings and perceptions. Thirdly, horticulture
has a direct tendency to turn the mind to God. It has
been truly said, that 'it presents to the bodies of children
healthful and placid muscular development; to their minds,
ever-varying proofs of the Almighty's greatness, goodness,
and wisdom.' Its advantages as an auxiliary to the general
work of such education as may fit the child for the station

in life in which it has pleased God to place him are borne
out, not merely by the practical proofs I have seen of its
efficiency, but by the highest authorities on the subject of
education, amongst whom are the Dean of Hereford and
my respected colleague, the Rev. Mr. Moseley, who says, in
one of his recent reports:—

The King's Sombourne School, on which I have already
reported at length, still stands alone in the views and principles
as to secular instruction on which it is conducted. Schools
resembling it in the scale of payment are indeed multiplying,
but the idea on which the school is based as to teaching, I find
reproduced nowhere. 'We educate,' said Mr. Dawes (now
Dean of Hereford), in his recent pamphlet, entitled *Observations on the Working of the Government Scheme of Education*, ' in the middle class with reference to the way in which
people are to get their livelihoods, and why not in the lower?'
That is a just view of the education, which considers it in relation
to the things which surround the child to be educated, and the
exigences of its condition, and so obvious a one, that it would
seem needless to insist upon it, were it not a very rare thing
to find it acted upon.

As to the manner of instruction, it suggests the expediency
of not dealing with a mind, subject to one class of moral influ-
ences, accustomed to expatiate among one class of objects,
and adapt itself to one social position, precisely as you would
a mind placed in all these respects under other circumstances
and in other relations.

All this obviously points to a different order of schools
than we at present possess, save in some exceptional cases.
It also demands another order of teacher. It is by more
intimate intercourse than that of the old style of mere master
and scholar that faults are known and corrected, virtues developed and nursed, sympathies strengthened, minds opened,
and knowledge improved. The field is a fine sphere for
effecting all this. I believe that schools without industrial
and moral training fulfil but part, and that the least important part, of education. It is not too much to say, that
mere schools cannot educate. I believe this to be true
even for the higher and middle classes of the people; but it

is infinitely more true and forcible when we are dealing with poor children, who require both moral and physical *régime*.

Of very little avail is it to teach such children the rudiments of book learning, or to seek to remedy evil passions and idle habits with catechisms and copy-books. They require, I repeat it, a far more apt and practical discipline, and I believe it is embodied in religious and ' industrial training.'

An aptitude for work of all kinds, and habits of industry, are the chief *industrial* advantages of the system. It is a mistake to suppose that the intention is to form finished labourers, or skilled artisans. Boys thus educated will probably, on leaving school, be neither able to plough, milk, shear, or mow; but they will, in addition to a store of practical and useful knowledge, have acquired those useful gifts— a handiness for work and a habit of industry. Mr. Bowyer, one of Her Majesty's Inspectors of Union Schools, speaks thus of many of the schools in workhouses; and assuredly it is quite as true and applicable to the majority of schools for the independent poor :—

They are reared like the sons of persons of fortune, and their days are passed in alternate lessons and play. A boy thus brought up is entirely unfitted for an agricultural labourer ; he can neither dig, hoe, nor plough ; is puzzled with a harness, and afraid of a horse. Any hard or continuous labour exhausts his body and wearies his mind ; he has formed a completely false conception of the life that awaited him ; instead of the joyous voices of his playfellows, he hears the rough commands of an unindulging master or a scolding mistress; he is continually reproached for his awkwardness and timidity, and reminded of his pauper origin. Under these circumstances, it can hardly be wondered at if he often look back with regret to the happy indolence of his childhood.

Vehrli, Principal of the Swiss Teachers' College at Con-
stance, thus expressed himself to Mr. Kay, the author of
that very valuable work, *The Social Condition of the People
in Germany and Switzerland* :—

After a long experience in teaching both the children of rich
and poor, it is my firm opinion that all children should be
accustomed, while they are young, to labour with their own
hands for a certain time every day. No school ought ever to
be situated in a town. All ought to be situated in the country ;
and every boy, no matter who his parents are, ought to be
obliged to labour upon the soil. Labour makes the children
healthy, capable of bearing fatigue, and robust, and it teaches
the children of the rich to get rid of all those notions which
riches are apt to stimulate ; to understand the feelings of the
poor better ; to treat them better, and to associate with them
better ; it thus diminishes the artificial distance between classes,
and, with the distinction of this artificial distance, it diminishes
also the jealous feelings which false mannerism on the part of
the rich too often engenders.

The beneficial effect of industrial labour on mental
activity is great. I have no hesitation in saying, that four
hours' school with it is quite equivalent to six without it,
and that more will be learned in the four hours ; for so
close is the sympathy of body with mind, that the indolence
of the one is the feebleness of the other. Mental strength,
incompatible with an inert frame, gains necessarily with
that which develops bodily vigour.

Vehrli's notions are much too far-going for adoption
here as regards the rich, but they are not beyond the
chance of being applied to the poor, which will suffice for
our purpose.

One of the best practical examples of the value of farm
schools is that of the school at Quatt in Shropshire, in
conjunction with the Bridgnorth Union, and now a district
school for the pauper children of four unions. This school
owes much of its merit and success to the unwearying
interest taken in it by Mr. Whitmore of Dudmaston, and
also to the peculiar talent and zeal of Mr. Garland, the

master, who has accomplished more by his own single-handed exertion, than could have been done by any one whose heart and hand were less devoted to the work. This school being a boarding-school, with many small children, requires much more labour than any day-school which adopted the industrial system. A short description of this school, as given in one of my reports to the Lords of the Committee of Council, will serve to illustrate the system recommended. It affords at once a proof of the profit both to the children and the ratepayers. It is the only school, with one or two exceptions, in my district, where the children are entirely separated from the workhouse. A private dwelling-house has been taken, in a rural village four miles from the workhouse, with about four acres of arable, and half an acre of meadow land. About fifteen boys cultivate this land, and attend to the stable, cows, pigs, &c. Not quite as many girls are instructed and employed in household work, sewing, baking, washing, and the dairy. The afternoons are wholly devoted to industrial labour, and the mornings chiefly to school instruction, in which the attainments of the children are very superior to those of most workhouse schools where no industrial training exists. An account of the produce of the land, together with the description given by Mr. Garland, the master, of his system of cultivation, was obtained by me from him, and has been extensively circulated throughout the unions of England. In that account, Mr. Garland gave an abstract of the ledger of one year, which has been made the subject of much comment and discussion. Further information on the subject will be found in the Appendix lettered C, which contains some authenticated details and proofs of the productiveness of spade husbandry, and to which I invite attention. It will suffice to state here, that this establishment is not based, as has been most erroneously supposed, on a self-supporting system : it was neither designed nor intended for such. The mere fact that only four and a half acres of land are taken into cultivation, ought to have prevented such a mis-impression. The large produce derived from this very limited portion of land has, indeed, been held forth, as well it might, as evidence of what may be done on a larger scale, in order to reimburse the expenses of such establishments ; but this was all.

The mis-impression was, however, of a somewhat mischievous tendency, inasmuch as it represented what is really a most successful attempt at industrial training, in the light of an agricultural speculation, of which the merits might be debateable. It may be safely upheld, as an almost perfect example of the virtues of spade husbandry for educational purposes, but it is by no means an example of all that may be effected in realizing large produce from the land by such a mode of cultivation. But I can safely aver, that the effects of the system at the Quatt farm school upon the minds, morals, hearts, and conduct of the children have left little to desire.

Although the children cannot of course learn all the various work to be done in farms, so as to become perfect labourers ; and though the girls in their various occupations in the house, the kitchen, the dairy, the bakehouse, the washhouse, and the laundry, do not in all cases become perfect servants ; yet both boys and girls learn the elements of profitable industry in all these useful spheres of service. They become apt, instead of inapt, for industrial pursuits. Instead of leaving the workhouses, as the children in them generally do,—nerveless, spiritless, inert, unskilled even in the use of their hands and arms, those at Quatt go forth well qualified to profit both themselves and those who employ them. This result seems to be fully appreciated by the farmers and others, who are desirous of obtaining them as servants.

Of their mental progress I can speak in equally high terms. The vigour of the body imparts itself to the intellect; and not only relieves the monotony of the school-room by the alternate labour in the fields, but it gives zest and energy to the powers of the mind.

In understanding the Scriptures, arithmetical calculations, the comprehension of the objects of nature, in general information, as well as in various branches of mere mechanical instruction, such as reading, writing, spelling, &c., these boys at the Quatt farm school excel those in the great majority of schools of far higher pretension which have fallen under my notice. Mr. Garland, the excellent master, has the faculty of gaining the affections of these poor children, many of whom in after life will regard him as a friend to whom they owe the highest debt of gratitude and affection.

The Rev. Mr. Moseley, speaking of this school, says:—

It is plain, therefore, that the fifteen boys of the Quatt school earn a good deal more than the cost of their dinners daily; and I think I am justified in assuming, that the like number of boys of similar ages, in any village school, aided by the master, having the same facilities for cultivating the same number of acres of ground, and devoting to the cultivation of it the same number of hours daily, might, in like manner, earn for themselves, and for three or four of the elder girls employed in the work of the dairy and the kitchen, a meal daily, of much humbler fare perhaps than that of the school of which I have spoken, but probably more substantial and more abundant than they could get at home.* It might improve with any improvement in the cultivation of the land, or with any increase in the industry of the little labourers. The value of improved methods of cultivation and greater industry could scarcely be brought home to them under any other form, indeed, in which they would be so likely to understand it. Whilst by this arrangement the training of the children in habits of forethought and industry would be provided for, the removal of a portion of the burden of their main-

---

* To be convinced of this, it is only necessary to inquire what kind of dinners poor children who live at a distance are accustomed to bring to eat at school.

tenance from the parent would probably secure their attendance
at school to a more advanced age.   Thus, what was sacrificed of
their school learning on the one hand, by setting apart only half
the day to it instead of the whole day, would be gained on the
other hand by their continuing at school longer.

The value of that moral influence which might, by a judicious
master, be exercised over the boys when associated with them
during their hours of labour and at their meals* will, I am sure,
be appreciated by every practical educationist.   It is during
these hours that the real characters of the children become
known, and at such times that the springs of action among them
may be influenced and controlled, and the public opinion of the
school brought over to the side of the schoolmaster.

I am well convinced of the entire truth of these opinions.

The profitableness of land cultivated as will be presently set forth in some detail has been found to be very
considerable wherever it has been properly tried.   There
are three reasons why it is so—

First,—The system of field gardening and high manuring
recommended is peculiarly adapted for boy labour, and
necessarily highly productive.

Secondly,—The labour is unpaid.

Thirdly,—The produce, instead of having to seek a market, is mainly consumed at home.

Market gardeners pay high rents; and, though they have
both to pay for labour, and also to seek a market, they make
good profits; *à fortiori*, school-farms would be more profitable.

---

* At the school of St. Mark's, Windsor, the boys breakfast with the
schoolmaster, each bringing his bread and butter, and the clergyman pro-
viding the cocoa.   I doubt not that this meal, eaten in common by the
teacher and children, has contributed largely to the high moral tone and
discipline of that remarkable school; and it is a great satisfaction to me
to find the opinion I hold on this subject supported by the experience of
so able and so devoted a friend to the education of the people as the Rev.
Stephen Hawtrey.   The most perfect idea we can form of a school
approaches most nearly to that of a well-ordered family, and, of the proper
relation of the teacher and his scholars, to that of a parent and his children.
It is, perhaps, difficult to conceive this idea to be realized unless they take
their meals together.

It is absolutely requisite to the successful working of the system, that the children *should partake of the produce of their labour.* There are instances of opposite systems— one at Hagley, in a school established there by Lord Lyttelton, and one by Lord Ellesmere at Worsley, at both of which the boys have the produce of the garden allotments attached to the school, and these work most successfully: In an other at Warren, established by the Countess Cawdor, which is the source of much benefit to the neighbourhood, the industrial department, comprising the cultivation of a few acres of arable land, does not thrive equally, the children having no part of the produce, and the parents not liking them to work. At Llanelly, a similar effort to introduce industrial employment proved abortive. I believe that the same feeling exists everywhere. The labouring classes set a just value on labour, and the constant objection made by them is, 'My child shan't work for nothing.' The only way of obviating this objection—and it is a very effectual one—is to give them something for their labour. Not only does this conciliate the parents, but it teaches the child an early lesson in the value of industry, and gives him a wholesome pride in the utility of his exertions. This is of great importance. It is of importance also in another way, touched on by the Rev. Mr. Moseley in the foregoing extract, namely, that it would prolong the attendance of the children in the school, reduced now throughout the kingdom by the parents to the shortest possible limit, from the universal desire and frequent necessity to set the children to earn something towards their livelihood as early as possible. Let schools be so moulded as to fulfil this desire instead of hindering it; let children be taught and worked together; let us abandon the purblind system of educating the head, and neglecting the hand and the heart, and our schools will soon be better filled, and our educational zeal better valued by the poor. As it is, I neither wonder a nor condemn their reluctance to surrender the time and labour-value of their children for the sort of instruction they chiefly obtain, and which they can but partially use, at the best, in after life.

The Rev. Mr. Mitchell also well observes, in his report in the *Minutes of Council* for 1848-9 :—

The employers of labour complain, either with reason or without, that the children attending national schools are unfitted for the work required of their condition ; and, therefore, occupiers of land generally are not merely indifferent, but frequently entirely opposed, to all education of the operative classes. The only method of overcoming this feeling, it seems to me, is to make the schools really practically efficient, by teaching in them such subjects only as may conduce to form the mind of a *labourer*, and fit him for his future career. And it should be borne in mind, that the education required by a town boy is widely different to that needed for an agricultural labourer. The object to be pursued is, to fit the child for his *present* occupation and status in society, not to *raise* him out of it. If he wishes to rise he must elevate himself. He must look to his own or his parents' exertions, not to the help of the State or charity, to place him in a more advanced position in life.

I am therefore led to think that, if it were possible to attach to every school land for the scholars to be trained in agricultural pursuits, it would be a very great improvement. The employers of labour would then see that a positive advantage was attained, and the parents might also be induced to make some further sacrifice to procure an evident worldly benefit, which, however it may be regretted, is to most of them the only, or at least chief, object why they send their children to school.

The same inspector corroborates and repeats these views in his report for 1850 :—

This system might be applied by means either of field-gardening or handicraft work. Where schools are so situate that ground cannot be had, much as it is to be preferred, handicrafts are the only resource. Many of the ragged schools have adopted them, and the boys learn shoemaking, tailoring, netting, &c. The great objection to this is, that these are trades over-full already ; and the second is, that they neither exercise the body, nor afford the means of moral training, so effectually as field-labour or gardening; and it is certainly quite impracticable to follow out Vehrli's plan of rural schools exclusively. In such cases, it is a great improvement over the present system to have any kind of industrial employment.

The kind of schools which appear to be best fitted for the wants of the times and the people having been thus briefly sketched, let us enter on the practical details and suggestions, not only for carrying the industrial system into effect, but likewise each branch of instruction, and the organization of ordinary schools for the poor, which will form the second part of this little work, bearing throughout the principle in view, that education, *in whatever branch*, to be of use must be thoroughly practical, and applicable to the business of life.

PART THE SECOND.

CHAPTER I.

The Building and Organization of Schools, &c.*

WHERE a school is to be built, the selection of a good site is very important. Where it can be avoided, a clayey or wet soil should never be selected. If the school is not intended to be industrial this is of less moment, as by building on arches, and attention to draining, the rooms may be kept dry, though it should be remembered —little as that fact is apparently regarded—that healthiness is as much dependent on soil as on almost any other circumstance of locality. If the school is to be a farm school, it *must* be on a loam or friable soil of some kind. A stiff clay soil is a very great objection; and none of the calculations hereafter given are capable of being verified on any other condition than that of a fair soil for the spade.

The buildings are in most cases far too ornamental and costly. It may well be questioned whether, when the funds exist for this outward show, it be not a very unwise example to set; and where some more essential matter is foregone in order to indulge in it, it is of course unjustifiable. This is, however, not unfrequently the case; and

---

* The mode of proceeding, in order to obtain a grant from the Committee of Council, will be best learned by writing to the secretary for the necessary forms of application.

when the school fittings are required, and the school teacher's salary to be determined, it is found that the fount of voluntary subscription has been exhausted on profitless expenditure, and the real requirements of the school are starved accordingly. This should not be. The only legitimate ornaments to a school should be sought within. A contrary practice, however, prevails; and if the present mongrel Gothic architecture is to pass muster for ornament, we oftener find it outside than inside. The taste thus generated becomes a precedent, and is obligatory almost as a law, much to the discouragement of poorer parishes and less opulent benevolence, deterred by examples of display they cannot imitate, and yet fear to dispense with. It would be a wholesome correction, if some rich philanthropists would build schools with perfectly plain walls, doors, and windows, supposing it possible to get a builder to assent to anything so heterodox.

The *Minutes of the Committee of Council,* for the years 1839-40, and also for 1844 and '45, contain several very good plans for school buildings.

To industrial schools, out-buildings should be attached adapted for the purpose, which will be more conveniently detailed hereafter, in treating of them specially.

THE ORGANIZATION AND FITTINGS.

These form a most important consideration. They may vary in some, but a small degree, according to the system of teaching pursued. Nevertheless, there are so many points of organization essential to all effective teaching, that a general plan may be laid down, almost equally applicable to any system. The suggestion of a new scheme of organization here would be not only unnecessary, but deteriorate the practical utility of this book, after the excellent and well-matured rules and plans recently put forth by the Committee of Council on Education, entitled, *Memorandum respecting the Organization of Schools in Parallel Groups of Benches and Desks.* As this publication is designed for circulation among the promoters of schools, that object will be in some degree furthered by its insertion here. It may be premised that, without such benches and desks no school can be deemed perfectly fitted. They are most essential.

MEMORANDUM, &c.

PRELIMINARY REMARKS.

Before a schoolroom is planned—and the observation applies equally to alterations in the internal fittings of an existing school-room, the number of children who are likely to occupy it ; the number of classes into which they ought to be grouped ; whether the school should be 'mixed,' or the boys and girls should be in different rooms—should be carefully considered, in order that the arrangements of the school may be designed accordingly.

A. Every class, when in operation, requires a separate teacher, be it only a monitor acting for the hour. Without some such provision it is impossible to keep all the children in a school actively employed at the same time.

The apprenticeship of pupil teachers, therefore, is merely an improved method of meeting what is, under any circumstances, a necessity of the case ; and, where such assistants are maintained at the public expense, it becomes of increased importance to furnish them with all the mechanical appliances that have been found by experience to be the best calculated to give effect to their services.

B. The main end to be attained is the concentration of the attention of the teacher upon his own separate class, and of the class upon its teacher, to the exclusion of distracting sounds and objects, and without obstruction to the head master's power of superintending the whole of the classes and their teachers. This concentration would be effected the most completely if each teacher held his class in a separate room ; but such an arrangement would be inconsistent with a proper superintendence, and would be open to other objections. The common schoolroom should, therefore, be fitted to realize, as nearly as may be, the combined advantages of isolation and of superintendence, without destroying its use for such purposes as may require a large apartment. The best shape (*see diagrams annexed*) is an oblong about eighteen feet in width. Groups of desks are arranged along one of the walls. Each group is divided from the adjacent group or groups by an alley, in which a light curtain can be drawn forward or back. Each class, when seated in a group of desks, is thus isolated on its sides from the rest of the school. The head master, seated at his desk placed against the opposite wall, or standing in front of any one of the classes, can easily superintend the school; while the separate teacher of each class stands in front of it, where the vacant floor allows him to place his easel for the suspension of diagrams and the use of the black board, or to draw out the children occasionally from their desks, and to instruct them standing for the sake of relief by a change in position. The seats at the desks *and* the vacant floor in front of each group are *both needed*, and should therefore *be allowed for* in calculating the space requisite for *each class*.

C. By drawing back the curtain between two groups of desks, the principal teacher can combine two classes into one for the purpose of a gallery lesson; or a gallery (doubling the depths of rows) may be substituted for one of the groups. For simultaneous instruction, such a gallery is better than the combination of two groups by the withdrawal of the intermediate curtain; because the combined width of the two groups is greater than will allow the teacher to command at a glance all the children sitting in the same line. It is advisable, therefore, always to provide a gallery.

The drawings annexed to the following rules purport simply to show the best internal dimensions of schoolrooms, and the best mode of fitting them up, the doors and windows being placed accordingly. The combination of such rooms with others of the same kind, with teachers' residences, and with the remainder of the school premises, as well as the elevations which may thereby be obtained, depending, as they always must, upon local circumstances, are not intended to be here shown.

The Committee of Council do not recommend that the benches and desks should be immovably fixed to the floor in any schools. They ought to be so constructed as to admit of being readily removed when necessary, but not so as to be easily pushed out of place by accident, or to be shaken by the movements of the children when seated at them.

The reasons of the following rules will be readily inferred from these preliminary explanations.

1. In planning a schoolroom, if it be not more than 18 feet in width, about 8 or 9 square feet will be sufficient for each child in actual attendance. If the width be greater, there must be a proportionate increase of area allotted to each child.

2. A school not receiving infants should generally be divided into at least four classes. (*The varying capacities of children*

between seven and thirteen years old will be found to require at least thus much subdivision.)

3. Parallel benches and desks, graduated according to the ages of the children, should be provided for all the scholars in actual attendance (*See Preliminary Remarks*, B.); and therefore a schoolroom should contain at least four groups of parallel benches and desks. (*See Rule* 2.)

4. A group should not contain more than three rows of benches and desks (*otherwise the distance of the last row is too great for the teacher to see the children's slates, and he must also raise his voice to a pitch which is exhausting to himself and adds inconveniently to the general noise.*)

5. As a general rule, no group of benches and desks should accommodate *more* than twenty-four children—*i. e.*, eight children in each of the three rows of the group, (*otherwise the width is too great. See Preliminary Remarks*, C.)

6. The proper lengths are 7 feet 6 inches for five children in a row ; 9 feet for 6 in a row ; 10 feet 6 inches for 7 in a row ; 12 feet for 8 in a row—*i. e.*, 18 inches for each child.
[The other dimensions and details are shown in the annexed drawings.]

7. Each group of desks must be separated from the contiguous group, either by an alley for the passage of the children, or by a space sufficient for drawing and withdrawing the curtains.
It will be sufficient to provide an alley for the passage of children *at one end only* of each group. At the other end a space of three inches will suffice for drawing and withdrawing the curtains.
[Alleys intended for the passage of children must not be less than 18 inches wide in the smallest school, and need not be more than 2 feet wide in any school, unless where a door or fireplace requires a greater interval.]

8. The best width for a schoolroom, intended to accommodate any number of children between 48 and 144, is 17 or 18 feet. This gives sufficient space for each group of benches and desks to be ranged (with its depth of three rows) along one wall, for the teachers to stand at a proper distance from their classes, and for the classes to be drawn out, when necessary, in front of the desks around the master or pupil teachers. (*No additional accommodation being gained by greater width in the room, the cost of such an increase in the dimensions is thrown away.*)

9. Where the number of children to be accommodated is too great for them to be arranged in five, or at most six, groups, an additional schoolroom should be built, and placed under the charge of an additional schoolmaster, who may, however, be subordinate to the head master, or a large school may be built.   Where neither of these arrangements can be accomplished, the schoolroom should not be less than 32 feet wide, and the groups should be arranged along both sides of the room, the children in all cases facing the centre. (*But such an arrangement is very inferior to that of the single row along one wall.   The opposite classes see each other, and their several teachers have to stand too close together. See Preliminary Remarks*, B.)

10. A curtain, capable of being readily drawn and withdrawn, should separate the several groups ; but not so as, when drawn, to project into the room more than 4 inches in front of the foremost desk.

11. If the schoolroom be lighted from above, which is the best possible mode, great care should be taken to prevent the skylights from leaking, and to provide channels for the water which the condensation of the children's breath will deposit on the inside of the glass.

12. All sashes, both upper and lower, should be hung ; and all windows, whether in the roof or elsewhere, should be made to open.

13. It is better to have a few large and well-placed windows than many small ones.

14. It is important to provide that the faces of the children and teachers, and also the black boards and diagrams, should be placed in a full clear light.

15. If the schoolroom be not lighted from above there should be windows, if possible, at each end and on one side of the room. The windows should be carried up as high as possible ; and those which are placed at the backs of the children, an arrangement which should be avoided as far as possible, should not come down within 5 feet 6 inches, or at least 5 feet, from the floor.

16. When the benches and desks are arranged on both sides of the room it should be lighted from above, or there should be, if possible, windows in *each* of the side walls.

17. Except when a schoolroom is very broad, there should be no fireplace in the centre of an end wall.
[A good place for a fireplace is under a window.]

BENCHES AND DESKS FIXED ON A RAISED PLATFORM.

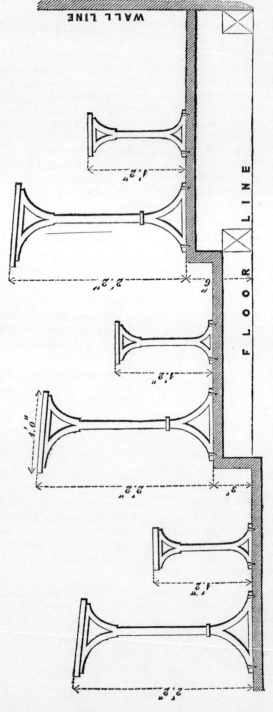

The dimensions in each of these three groups are calculated for children of the age of from 11 to 13. It is important that the dimensions should be varied to suit younger children.

** There are other Plans in the *Memorandum*, a selection from which is given here.

PLAN OF BENCHES AND DESKS.

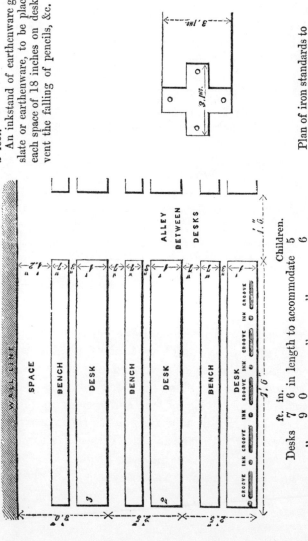

Alleys between groups of Desks, from 1 foot 6 inches to 2 feet.

An inkstand of earthenware glazed, with sliding covers of slate or earthenware, to be placed at the extreme right of each desk. The grooves are to prevent the falling of pencils, &c.

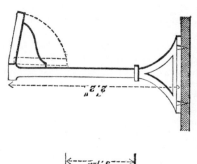

Plan of iron standards to Desks and Benches.

The flap of the Girls' Desks made to fall down for needle-work.

		ft.	in.			Children.
Desks		7	6	in length to accommodate	5
,,		9	0	,,	,,	6
,,		10	6	,,	,,	7
,,		12	0	,,	,,	8

18. The desks should be either quite flat or *very slightly* inclined. The objections to the inclined desk are, that pencils, pens, &c., are constantly slipping from it, and that it cannot be conveniently used as a table. The objection to the flat desk is, that it obliges the children to stoop. A raised ledge in front of a desk interferes with the arm in writing.

19. A large gallery for the simultaneous instruction of two or more classes, without desks, may advantageously be provided in a classroom, or at one end of the schoolroom. Such a gallery may be better placed along, than across, the end of the school-room, for the reasons stated in the Preliminary Remarks, B.

20. No such gallery, nor any gallery in an infant schoolroom, should be placed in front of a window, unless it be very high up above the heads of the children when they stand on the top row of the gallery.

21. No infant gallery should hold more than 80 or 90 infants.

22. An infant school should (besides a large gallery) have a small group of benches and desks for the occasional use of the elder infants.

23. The alleys leading to a gallery should be at its sides, not in its centre. (*See Rules 5 and 6.*)

24. Great care should be taken that the valves which admit the fresh air into the schoolroom should be placed so as not to create draft where the teachers and children sit.

25. An easel and a black board should be provided for each class, and a larger black board for the gallery.

VENTILATION AND DRAINAGE.

Nothing is more important than attention to these essential points. There should in every school be an inlet vent below, and an outlet vent above. This is easily accomplished by means of perforated zinc plates. Oil-curtain ventilators in the chimney, near the ceiling, are admirably adapted for letting off foul, and keeping up the circulation of fresh air, in any apartment, the warm in the chimney causing the draft, and the little curtains preventing the escape of smoke into the room. Many a close room has been rendered wholesome by this cheap and simple expedient. In a school, or other crowded room, this, however, though an admirable assistant, could not suffice for the outlet vent.

Drainage is equally essential. It is the established usage, in perhaps two-thirds of the houses in this country, to pen up the stuff which flows from them in holes and cesspools close under the noses of the occupants. These abominations are usually constructed, even when walled, so as to allow of the escape of the liquid, which penetrates through the bricks, and saturates the surrounding soil, which of course exhales its effluvia into the air, and is frequently the hidden cause of disease. This plan is in one view both cheap and nasty, for it avoids the necessity of emptying these places out. It is, however, less economical than at first appears, for the value derivable from the contents of the cesspool for raising garden or farm produce is entirely lost, and the plan results in an injury to the health at the expense of the pocket.

Where schools have ground or garden attached, there should always be a tank, properly cemented as hereafter described, into which everything runs, and from which it is again pumped and put on the land, the drains from the building being properly secured. Where the school-house is deprived of the advantage of land, the refuse, &c., cannot be carried away too far. It should be conveyed into some culvert or drain, entirely away from the house if practicable; if not, a cemented tank should be sunk, with properly-fitted stink-traps, and so constructed with man-trap above, as to admit of being emptied when full. Where neither of these is done, health is certain to be more or less injured.

Warming stoves are more economical than open fires, but never so healthy.

THE COST AND SIZE OF SCHOOL BUILDINGS.

It is very difficult to give an estimate which is of any practical use, so much must depend on the locality, the character of the materials, the fittings, and the style of building. In few cases can what is requisite for the schoolrooms alone be furnished for 100 children at so little as £200, site not included; for 150 or 200, the cost would be less in proportion. Small schools are always the dearest, and generally the least efficient. Too large ones are, however, an evil. It is doubtful whether 250 is not the maximum which can be ever properly superintended by the same master and mistress.

The height of the room, from the floor to the wall-plate, should be from 10 to 15 feet, according to its dimensions. Schoolrooms surrounded by other buildings should be somewhat more lofty than those in open situations, in order to admit a greater body of air.

DOORS AND WINDOWS.

The door at which the children enter should always have a porch, under which they may shelter themselves in case of rain, or whilst kept waiting. It is also desirable for the marching exercises, that all the doors should be made to open *outwards*. Windows should be on opposite sides of the room and high up.

CLASS-ROOM, HATS, ETC.

In a school for 100 children the classroom should be at least 10 feet by 12, and 15 by 18 would be better. It should have a small gallery, capable of containing from thirty to forty children; the hats and cloaks also may be hung up here, or the main gallery may be so arranged as to allow of their being placed under it, or they may be hung up in the porch, if that be convenient: at all events they should not, when it can be avoided, be hung round the main schoolroom.   Many teachers like to have the children enter through the classroom, instead of entering directly through the main schoolroom; the arrangement may be easily made by an extra door, and has its advantages.   Moderately large schools should have two class-rooms, as before observed.

Of course, where the funds cannot be had, there are less costly modes of housing schools.   The Home and Colonial Society, in their admirable *Hints on the Establishment of Schools*, from which some of the foregoing particulars are borrowed, very justly remark that—

Two cottages standing together, the rooms on the ground-floor (if sufficiently lofty) thrown into one, a room up-stairs appropriated for a classroom, and the remaining rooms as a residence for the teacher, the garden forming a play-ground; or a barn with the walls whitewashed, and the tiles pointed (not ceiled, as that often causes echo), and when large enough, a portion divided off for a classroom, will be frequently found to answer the desired purpose.   In the latter case, a residence for the teacher should be procured very near to the school, as this is a matter never to be lost sight of.   Of course it is unnecessary to point out the advantage of using Sunday schoolrooms for infant schools during the week, when they can be obtained; and if there be no classroom attached, a division of the schoolroom by a woollen curtain will often be found both more convenient and cheaper than a wooden partition.

BOOKS AND MAPS AND APPARATUS.

Schools under inspection may obtain grants of any school-books in the list of the Committee of Council on Education at about two-thirds of the usual selling price.   The list of books is a very full and good one.   The conditions under which the grant may be obtained, are to be had, like all the other forms, on application in writing to the Secretary of the Committee.   The books deemed most useful will be indicated under each branch of instruction in the following pages.   Maps of the British Islands and Palestine are indispensable in every school.   Those of Europe and the world ought to be added.   The exceedingly low rate at which these, and all school books, are now supplied, put it in the power of the poorest promoters to obtain at least a moderate supply.

The apparatus needed in schools is very slight; with a proper arrangement of forms and desks, two black boards on frames and castors, will answer every purpose of ordinary illustration.   Small working models of the mechanical powers are also necessary for the more advanced classes, and are strongly to be recommended, though as yet but rarely introduced.   At Lord Lyttelton's school at Hagley they have been long used with excellent effect; to these, working models of pumps, steam-engines, looms, cranes, &c., may be most advantageously added, together with models of mines and strata for mineral districts, where it is useful to give the boys some insight into the nature of their probable occupation.   This principle of adapting the instruction and its instruments to the probable wants of the scholars should be the guiding principle.   The raised platform (see plan, p. 58) will serve as a gallery.   It is invaluable.

PLAYGROUNDS.

These are essential where there is no ground or garden, and a useful addition where there is.   They serve, to some extent, as a means of moral training, and nurseries of character, as well as for bodily exercise and muscular training.   Mr. Stow calls it 'the uncovered schoolroom.'

It should be as large as conveniently practicable, and so floored that it may be soon dry after rain.   Small borders for flowers should, if possible, be placed round it.   One of the best floors for playgrounds is a binding gravel, and a portion of it turfed, on which the common circular swings and the following bars, &c., may be advantageously placed, so that the tumbles may be soft.

1. *The Climbing Stand.*

The exertion of raising the body by the hands, moving them up these ropes, is extremely healthful, tending to exert the muscles to the best advantage.

2. *The Parallel Bars.*

The exercises on these bars consist in supporting the body on the arms, one hand resting on each bar, and by moving each hand alternately, proceeding forwards and backwards along the bars; in swinging the body between the arms; and in springing over the bar on each side, both backwards and forwards.

3. *The Horizontal Bar*

consists of a wooden bar formed of some tough wood, not apt to splinter or warp, about three inches in diameter, and usually six feet long, turned or planed round and smooth, in order that the hands may not be blistered by the friction.

The Circular Swing is well understood. It is discommended, however, by one of the school societies, because accidents have sometimes happened. It were difficult to mention any athletic exercise at which accidents may not happen. This is, in my opinion, a recommendation of them. The object of all these exercises is to prepare children for the incidents of life, and especially those of hard-working life. If they are to be carefully guarded from such dangers as ordinary care may avoid, they are, in so far, *not* being prepared for the incidents of their future life. It is essential that they should, on the contrary, be early introduced to such dangers, and experienced in them, and in the means of avoiding them. We should, of all things, take care not to rear apron-string children on the go-cart system.

CHAPTER II.

Systems of Teaching.

THE importance of systems has been greatly over-rated. There are very good and very bad schools in each system. The best schools are usually on no system, but adopt the best parts of each. Most modes of teaching have ceased to be peculiar to the systems in which they originated.

Galleries, for example, are happily no longer an adjunct only of infant schools, but their admirable utility for all simultaneous and collective instruction is generally appreciated. The addition to them of desks relieves another part of the school-room from that encumbrance, without in the least degree lessening the value of the gallery. This is a great improvement. The system of separate class instruction, as well, is indispensable; and accordingly, in all good schools, room is left on the floor for their formation. This should never be neglected. If this view continues to be adopted, we shall soon see the systems disappear which either fill the area of school-rooms with parallel benches and desks, with a meagre margin for drafts (according to the British), or with the formal parallelograms of benches, giving nearly the whole area to classes, and a writing-desk, fixed like a shelf round the wall, where the children are placed with their backs to their masters, like horses at mangers.

All these points are rather important; but after all, as is well said by Mr. Kennedy in a recent report, 'What is wanted in every school is a *master mind*. With an inferior schoolmaster, *no method will be good,* and with a really good one, *no system will be bad.*' So thinks also Professor Moseley: 'Nothing,' he says, 'has been more certainly impressed on my mind, by an experience in the inspection of schools, now extending over six years, than the fact that the whole question of elementary education is involved in a gradual elevation of the religious and moral character, and of the intellectual standard of the teachers.'*

On the most important work of imparting knowledge, and educating the mind of the child, it may be remarked, that all modes may be reduced to two leading features— first, to expound, and second, to question: first, to put knowledge into the head of the scholar, and then to find out whether the head has got possession of it. This is best done by such expositions of the subject as may be at once the most intelligible and *the most attractive.* This is highly important. The teacher who does not choose or cannot interest the scholars in what they learn, and relieve lessons of the repugnant dryness they have hitherto been clothed with, is not fit to be a teacher at all. He must enter into the child's mind, and consult his taste as well as inform his ignorance. Then comes close questioning, which tests the progress made, and makes the work secure. It is on the skill of the teacher, however, in doing this, that the whole benefit of the system depends. No set rules can dictate what to explain, how to elucidate, or how to question. Still less can the life and spirit, so essential to good teaching, be imparted by precepts. If the master has not the necessary qualities, it is of but little use to endeavour to instil them into him.

Taking these general principles as the basis of our remarks, let us see how far the chief component parts of each system are available.

PUPIL-TEACHERS AND THE MONITORIAL SYSTEM.

The monitorial system, of all others, requires a first-rate teacher; and so far from saving him any trouble, if this

---

* *Minutes* for 1848-49-50; vol. i. p. 19.

system is to be efficiently carried out and prevented from being a perfect infliction on the school, it will greatly increase his work. Dunn, the chief and ablest advocate of the system, adopts De Fellenberg's words, and affirms that it requires 'a vigilance that never sleeps, a perseverance that never tires.' Mr. Crossley, the zealous, highly-skilled superintendent at the Borough-road, has given the following detail of the duties incumbent on the master of a monitorial school, which I transcribe, not merely for the sake of showing how thoroughly impossible it is to secure command of such functions in at least nine-tenths of our existing school teachers, even if they had the time for them. I give it also for the more important purpose of affording an admirable summary of the proper training of *pupil-teachers*, to which I think nearly all of the following directions is appropriate :—

A master's first thoughts, on taking charge of a school, should be directed to the formation of a band of monitors. For this purpose, after selecting, as nearly as he can, boys possessing suitable qualities, he will arrange his lessons according to the number of his drafts, which will of course depend on the number of his pupils. Having thus determined on *the number of his drafts*, and on the lessons to be studied at *each* draft, he will appoint a boy to the several stations to act as a monitor. The boy thus appointed, is supposed to be able to spell and to read the lessons, but possessing no knowledge of the business beyond these two qualifications; he is then first to be taught the meaning of each word, and to be exercised in giving illustrations of its varied application, both from Scripture, general history, science, and from subjects within the range of the pupils' observation. In some cases the prefixes, postfixes, and roots of the words are important. He must then be exercised in *the art of questioning*, so as to be able to communicate his information by interrogation, and by that alone, and to keep up, without any auxiliary stimulant, the eager attention of his pupil. He must further be taught to vary his questions on the same word, so that repetition may not tire ; and he must be instructed how to discover the proper instant to change from simultaneous repetition to individual examination, from brief description to rapid questioning, from the lively statement of facts, to the calm and impressive deduction of instructive lessons.

In giving definitions, the *simplest* mode of expression must be carefully sought; which will, of course, generally be in Saxon phraseology. These definitions must be learned by the newly-appointed monitors at the rate of about a dozen or twenty a day. The master must set apart a portion of each day, either from 12 to 1 (which usually is best), or from 6 to 7 in the evening, to hear each individual repeat these meanings. In the first instance, it may be necessary to give up both these portions of time to the work. To accomplish his purpose, he must form his newly-selected monitors into a draft; each in turn must then question on his own particular words, as he would do in the draft for which he is training. After the definition has been given, the questioner for the time being must call for an instance of the application of the word, or an illustration containing some additional information more or less remotely connected with it. Here the master's reading, experience, and judgment will find full scope; for when the boys fail, he should be ready to supply the desirable lesson, the parallel passage, the fact, or the opinion. In this way the monitor's mind is stored with numerous pertinent illustrations: he is exercised in applying them naturally, and in familiar language; and instead of communicating in a formal manner and set style, he learns so to vary his observations as to avoid sameness. His mind thus disciplined, will ever furnish him with new examples in his daily course of teaching. This plan must be followed daily till the whole of the lessons of each draft have been the subject of inquiry; nor must this practice be discontinued, until monitors can be chosen from among the boys who have themselves been taught by those who have thus been trained.

I must, however, here enter a protest against the master's supposing that all is done when his monitors are trained; and, further, against his even imagining that they ever will be thoroughly trained by this or by any other method, except he can and does set them the example, both in the manner and in the spirit of teaching. *He must, from the commencement, be daily seen teaching in the drafts, infusing into his monitors a spirit little short of enthusiasm, and showing himself a model both of what he wishes them to be and to do.*

Mr. Dunn, with great truth, thinks that the difficulties of his office do not stop here.

Severer trials (he says) than any that have yet been mentioned, must occasionally be endured by the conscientious teacher of a monitorial school,—I mean those which are connected with the punishment, and, if necessary, the dismissal of his monitors.

I have already referred to the opportunity which extended responsibility affords, for the *manifestation* of *evil* as well as good principles, and I have ranked this means of discovering character among the advantages of the monitorial system. It is obvious, however, that it can only be so in proportion as delinquency thus manifested is followed by appropriate punishment. Monitors, by their office, are exposed to certain temptations from which others are exempt. Bribes of various kinds, in spite of every regulation to the contrary, will from time to time be offered and accepted. Partiality will then be shown to one, and tyranny be exercised over another; falsehood will probably follow, and evils of the most tremendous character may in this way be fostered and indulged. It must be so while human nature continues as it is.*

It must indeed. And inasmuch as the few boys old enough to be monitors in the great bulk of our schools are open to all these evil dispositions, and not one schoolmaster out of one hundred can or will take the prescribed pains to counteract them, it follows clearly enough that no benefit is derivable from the monitorial system in our schools for the poor which is not counterbalanced by the risk of very great evils. The bullying and bribery may be chiefly confined to large schools, but the worthlessness of the instruction given by the majority of the monitors is unfortunately but too prevalent, as I am well able to vouch. Supposing that the intense training and incessant watching can be effected, the monitorial system presents these advantages—viz., it trains teachers; it gives to those taught the probably greater sympathy with, and comprehension of, their difficulties; it promotes industry, and tends to enhance its importance in the eyes of the school; it is also said to be economical, inasmuch as there is no payment of salaries.

Weighing, however, the advantages against the evils, I incline to regard the monitorial system merely as a resource in default of all other means of maintaining a school.

Every single advantage it offers may be derived from pupil-teachers, with these great additional benefits—first,

* Dunn's *Principles of Teaching*, p. 55.

that being far more discriminately selected, they are qualified, morally and mentally, for the work; secondly, and that
there being fewer of them, the master has more opportunity
and power to instruct and superintend them; thirdly, that
he being paid to do so, is more likely to do it well; fourthly,
that the expense does not fall on the school, but on the
State; fifthly, that all such schools are inspected, and enjoy,
therefore, a further security that the pupil-teachers will be
well trained.

Without going the length of saying that monitors should
never be employed in any school, I think that the primary
effort of *every* school should be to do without them, and to
effect the same object by pupil-teachers; and where that is
impracticable, at least by efficiency in the schoolmaster. I
have seen a mixed school of eighty children thoroughly well
taught by one master and a single assistant teacher. At
the Quatt Union School, sixty-five boys and girls have been
well instructed by one master, who at the same time trained
fifteen of the boys in spade husbandry. If the master has,
in fact, both zeal and skill, no monitor or even pupil-
teacher is required for a moderately sized school. It is
scarcely possible, however, to overrate the value of pupil-
teachers, not only to the schools in which they are now
placed, but far more to those schools for which they will
hereafter form a supply of competent teachers. The only
danger to be avoided is, lest in the natural desire to fill the
office, both on the part of the candidates and of the inspector, appointments should take place rather more rapidly
than is consistent with competency. Time, however, will
soon cure this.

The great object in all instruction being to conquer
the natural inattention of the child, and to make him
thoroughly understand what he ought to learn, all the
modes of imparting knowledge have been devised for this
purpose, and ought to be estimated accordingly.

The gallery lessons form a new era in education, and
are admirably adapted to give effect to each of these
modes.   Of these the synthetical method combined with
the simultaneous has perhaps proved to be the most
efficient.   In explaining and describing, the teacher, adopting such phrases and illustrations as are most familiar to
the children, leads them from the known to the unknown
by easy and imperceptible steps ; and to borrow the words
of Mr. (now Sir James) Kay Shuttleworth, ' to render the
knowledge of general facts the consequence of an acquaintance with the elements from which they spring.'   Thus
the children in a measure teach themselves by a process of
deduction, and their reason is thus exercised whilst the
mind is informed.   Then comes the questioning, which,
if it be efficiently done, will combine direct questions
with elliptical statements.   Mr. Stowe recommends the
combination of the two ; ' sometimes a question, then
sometimes an ellipsis; keeping in view the age and attainments of the children.   The younger the children are, the
more frequently must an ellipsis be formed.   The question
sets the mind a-thinking or astir, the ellipsis draws out
what has been set a-moving.   The union of the two, along
with analogy and illustration, form intellectual training.'
Most of our readers are familiar with the elliptical system,
but will excuse this fragmentary illustration of it, mixed
with questions, for the benefit of those who may not.

SUBJECT.—*The Pharisees watching our Lord on the Sabbath-day*.
          [The children's answers are in *italics*.]
Who were the Pharisees?
*Self-righteous Jews; great hypocrites, &c. People who pretended
to be holier than they were.   Men who trusted to outward forms
of religion, and prided themselves on that, but who were, in
reality, haughty and wicked, &c.**

---

* The teacher should generally require more than one answer.   It
exercises the reflection, and enables the children to enter into a wholesome emulation with each other.
No ellipsis should ever be made *in a question;* only in statements.

Teacher: Then they were not what they seemed, but——
hypocrites, liars, pretenders, &c.

Teacher: Very true, they were——*hypocrites*——people who, too like many in these times, say one——*thing*——while they——*mean another.*

Teacher: Just so. Now tell me in which of the parables are their vainglory and self-righteousness described?
The parable of the Publican and Pharisee praying in the Temple.

Teacher: They made long——*prayers*——then, to be seen ——*of men.*

Teacher: Of what was it that the Pharisees wished to accuse our blessed Lord, as described in the passage we have just read?
Of breaking the Sabbath-day.

Teacher: Because he healed——*the man with a withered hand.*

Teacher: Was it for love of God that they did this?
No.

Teacher: No; it was through hatred of——*Christ.*

Teacher: Yes; in order that they might——*kill him.*

Teacher: Did Christ really break God's law?
No.

Teacher: Certainly; for according to the spiritual meaning, it is lawful to do——*good on the Sabbath-day.*

Questioning and answering should be both simultaneous and individual. Neither of these is necessarily confined either to the gallery or the class, as is often supposed, but both are applicable to each. Simultaneous questions and answers are more useful when they follow individual ones, as a means of reimpressing them on the minds and memory of the whole class or gallery. To use the simultaneous mode alone, is almost inevitably to neglect the bulk of the children, who readily catch and repeat the answers of the few most forward ones, and are soon able to do so with a rapidity and apparent simultaneousness which impose a belief that they are really instructed, whilst they are answering mechanically, like parrots. The only way to prevent this is to question individually.

The best mode of questioning and answering individually, is to make all the children who think they can

answer the question hold out their hands, silently, as soon
as it is put.   The teacher will then name the child who is
to answer it, usually selecting one who is least likely to
answer it rightly and fully.   When the answer is given, all
the other children who are holding their hands out *and
intended to give the same answer, drop theirs;* they who
intended to give another answer, or a fuller and more
complete one, on the contrary, continue to hold their hands
out ; and the teacher then again selects one of these to
give his answer.   And so on, on the same system, until all
the hands are down, and all the answers are exhausted.
The intelligent teacher, or rather, the teacher who is up to
his craft, will point out errors, and having put in proper
phrase the cream of the answers, will then explain it to
the whole class, and question on it generally, getting
answers simultaneously.   Of course it is not designed to
lay down this as the only course to be pursued, but as an
illustration of one, and perhaps the chief, mode in which
the explanatory and questioning part of instruction may
be given.

From what has been said, it will be more apparent that
a mixed system is feasible and expedient.   All systems
resolve themselves into different modes of applying one of
the two main kinds of instruction—the oral or explanatory, and the catechetical ; the one to convey knowledge to
the mind, the other to keep it there.

In 'Object lessons,' as they are improperly named, the
'objects' ought to be merely incidental to ' lessons,' and
are not a distinct branch of instruction, or of a system.
They are essential to any system which aims at giving the
children a thorough comprehension of what they learn,
especially on subjects of every-day knowledge and the
arts of life.   They ought at first to consist of simple
substances, such as chalk, oak, marble; and then of simple
manufactures and compounds, a clasp-knife, a plane, a bell,

brass, cheese, soap, &c., and so on, to the most compound and complex, such as the printing-press, steam-engine, &c. In these, the black board is indispensable. In all such lessons, the rules above-cited from Mr. Crossley as to the mode of explanation are most important; they should be closely observed.

Lessons on animals are also of the same character, a picture of the animal being placed before the children. The following synopsis of such a lesson, taken from the daily lesson-book of the British and Foreign Society, will exemplify what is meant.

Polar Bear.

Polar Bear.—Show picture—quadruped,—12 feet long—hair white—long—coarse—shaggy; —foot, plantigrade; teeth, incisors—canine—molares.

1. *Abode.*—Greenland—islands of ice—frozen ocean—show on map—poles—cold—ice—snow; other animals there—seals, fish, &c.
2. *Character and habits.*—Powerful—savage—ferocious—great activity in water—can swim 6 or 7 leagues at sea—omnivorous—chiefly fish and blubber; love of young —(*illustration*) sailors and bear.
3. *How caught.* — Tracked by dogs — killed with guns—speared.
4. *Uses.*—Skin—shoes, &c., as leather; flesh, food for Greenlanders—fat, melted—oil—tendons, thread for Greenlanders.

Lesson.—Wisdom of God in adapting animals to different countries—white hair—cold—(*illustration*) pieces of cloth on snow in the sun—wants of the Greenlanders supplied.

The various subjects touched on show how these lessons may be made to combine instruction, not only in the precise subject of what has been read or explained, but of a vast amount of collateral and pertinent knowledge, partly relating to geography, trade, natural history, manufactures, national character, and lastly, to religion itself.

All these lessons should be got up by the teacher beforehand, whose great aim should be to bring to the work a full head.

Lessons on particular branches of instruction are very needful, and hints on each will follow this; but it is all-important to give collective lessons which shall embrace, more or less, all elementary subjects. These, though they can be given very fairly and usefully in classes—say, two classes combined—yet the best way of giving them is to the whole school, or as large a number as can be conveniently congregated in the gallery. Many of the younger children, who will be unable to follow the whole, will yet glean a good deal; and if the lesson be given with due animation, will be at once usefully interested, and by degrees trained to take their part in it. Besides, it is an excellent opportunity of training in discipline, obedience, and attention. For the elder children, the collective lesson is invaluable. Here it is that the master can effectually deal with the minds of the children—pour knowledge broadside into them; evoke their latent powers of thought, reason, and expression; correct errors, develop and apply intellectual activity, while he quickens and moulds the moral sense.

There is a danger to which the gallery leads, which should be named: it is that of affording great facility to the trickery of got-up exhibitions, by means of cramming a few children scattered over the gallery, so as to astound visitors with their answers, and give a false colour to the school. The Rev. Mr. Brookfield remarks:—'These examinations have, however, been much simplified by the expert assistance of the clergy, and by their disdain of those annual impostures which consume time merely in putting into the children's mouths a mechanical series of answers to amaze a Midsummer row of visitors not acquainted with the secret.' There is no other corrective. Such frauds ought to be treated as gross immoralities, and exposed and denounced accordingly. It is an abuse to which gallery examinations are necessarily liable; and it must be left to the more intelligent part of the auditors to test the reality of such exhibitions by putting *simple questions of their own* to the children, both collectively and individually. This is the only safeguard; for the instances are nowise rare where the teacher is sufficiently unprincipled to resort to this mean and mischievous device, of which the direct effect is to give the whole school a lesson of deceit.

THE TRI-PARTITE SYSTEM.

The Rev. Mr. Moseley has recommended this excellent plan, which was in use in Scotland some years ago, of which we will give a slight sketch. He proposes to class the following subjects thus:—

A. For oral instruction.
B. For writing, and slate arithmetic.
C. For reading.

And to each of these subjects he assigns a separate place, or gallery, divided by a curtain, as pointed out in the following sketch:—

Hours.	I.	II.	III.
9 to 10	A	B	C
10 to 11	B	C	A
11 to 12	C	A	B

Mr. Moseley also proposes that the children should be formed into three equal divisions, and that when the morning prayers and Bible lessons are terminated, each class should go into one of these localities, and there receive the instruction belonging to that locality. Thus, while Division I. are occupied with oral instruction, Division II. will be engaged in writing and arithmetic, and Division III., in subdivisions of from six to ten, in reading under pupil-teachers and monitors.

In the foregoing sketch, three hours in the morning are devoted to school, and, in the summer, three hours in the afternoon.

At the expiration of each hour, a change is made: No. 1, who were receiving oral instruction, are removed to No. 2 for writing and arithmetic; and No. 2 are removed on to No. 3 for reading; while No. 3 go to the master to be examined in the reading lesson they have just had.

The great benefit derived from this system is, that it is much less noisy in the school, one class only receiving oral instruction at the same time, whilst two are employed in silent occupations.

CLASS-ROOMS.

These are used under any system of teaching for the instruction usually of the older scholars, and especially of pupil-teachers, in the higher branches of distinct subjects. They are, of course, less needed in small and elementary schools, but are more or less useful in all.

———

In this brief summary of systems, and hints rather for their successful combination than respective preference, enough has been said in this place. It has been deemed desirable to condense, rather than to enlarge, a subject which certainly has, in the opinion of the best judges, obtained undue importance and attention. It is of much greater importance to note well the predominating faculties of each child, and to teach him accordingly, always observing the rule of what will be most useful to him or her in after-life.

Surely, it is time to adapt education to capacities, and to modify it accordingly; instead of treating children like bricks, who only want to be cast in one mould, to be turned out all alike for the same use.

CHAPTER III.

How to Teach Reading, Writing, and Ciphering.

GOOD reading is as much neglected as any branch of elementary instruction. It is deemed quite enough, in a large majority of schools, that the children should be able to utter the words they see before them without emphasis or expression. It is certainly in exceptional cases only that the latter acquirements are thought necessary, or even desirable. That good impressive reading is not among the most essential acquirements for a poor child, and that it will be but occasionally useful to him in after life, cannot be denied; still it is always important that what is taught at all should be taught well; and it is equally so that it should be taught with the least possible expenditure of time. The ordinary mode of teaching it is the longest; and it is one of the leading defects of bad schools to keep the youngest children wading through the alphabet, and stumbling through columns of unmeaning monosyllables, till they are half stupified and thoroughly disgusted with the whole process. Nothing can be better calculated to make a young child regard 'lessons' as the great grievance of his life—a feeling which he not unfrequently or unnaturally transfers to the other steps in his educational career.

There is no occasion that the child should learn the alphabet as a set lesson at all. The order of the letters (which is wholly without arrangement or classification) is not a necessary acquirement at an early age, and of extremely limited use in after life for children who will not use dictionaries. Then as to the letters in combination, unfortunately in our language to learn the sound of most of them gives no help whatever as to their sound in different words, and therefore often misleads in reading. For instance, the child is taught that *b, a,* is to be sounded as *ba* (long), this misteaches him at once to pronounce *bad* and *mad* similarly as *bade, made,* and he has then to unlearn what he has been taught at great sacrifice of time and pains and inclination. In fact, he has been disgusted and prejudiced against education itself by a drudgery, which so far from being useful, is absolutely useless. There are high authorities for this view.

The Central Society of Education, which some years since enrolled the most distinguished friends of education among its members, in one of its publications says :—

It is not our wish that children should any longer conquer this ' most difficult of human attainments' (reading) through the medium of A, B, C; a, b, ab; b, a, ba, &c., neither would we encounter with them any system of syllabic classifications, on which several meritorious elementary reading-books have been recently published; and the naming of the letters, as in spelling, we would altogether discard. A modification of the system of Jacotot, with a series of interesting lessons printed so large that all the children could see them, would be found to be the only needful auxiliaries to be employed. The lessons must be graduated, and every sentence contained in them must possess a meaning level to the comprehension of the children. Monosyllabic lessons, though almost universally employed in early teaching, are not of that value which is generally attached to them; indeed, such lessons are so filled with particles,—words which only possess a meaning in connexion with others,—and so deficient of the language of ordinary life, that they have less interest for children than exercises apparently more difficult, but which are less cramped and more natural.

The American President of the Nashville University, Lindsley, in an excellent lecture on education, remarks that—

In order to learn to read, it is by no means indispensable that the long, tedious method of the schools for children should be adopted : the process may be rendered extremely simple and easy. It is not necessary to commence even with the alphabet, or to go through a course of spelling in Dilworth or Webster. Adults have very recently been taught to read in penitentiaries, and elsewhere, in a very short period,—even within one or two weeks, in some cases,—who previously did not know a letter. The chaplain, or teacher, opens his Bible, directs the eye of his pupil to the first verse of the first chapter, reads it distinctly, points out each *word* to the learner, and makes him repeat it,— and so on to the end of the verse : in a few minutes the pupil can read the verse backwards or forwards. He now knows the *words* by their *phases* or *appearances* in the book.

Mr. Henry Dunn, enlarging on the necessity of annexing sense to sound, and making the child comprehend whatever he utters, observes, in his 'Principles of Teaching:'—

The great evil of putting before children unmeaning combinations of letters, such as 'bla, ble, bli, blo, blu,' and all the rest of this ridiculous tribe, is, that in reading them, a *habit* is formed of separating the sight and sound of words from sense, a habit which frequently cleaves to the mind long after the days of childhood have passed away.

*   *   *   *   *   *   *

The alphabet is usually the first subject presented to the notice of a child at school; and a more difficult or tiresome lesson he is never doomed to meet with in his whole future course. The *names* of the letters are unmeaning and arbitrary sounds; and, with two or three exceptions, the *forms* are not associated with any object previously recognised. How can such an exercise be expected to produce anything but weariness and disgust ?

Mr. Woodbridge thus forcibly illustrates the same mistaken system :—

The absurdity of teaching the letters of the alphabet by their arbitrary *names*, in place of their *sounds*, has long been felt in France and Germany. We tell a child to say *pe-aytch-wi-es-i-see*, and then call upon him to pronounce it. What would he conclude, if he reasoned, but that it must be *peaytchwiesisee*, and by what magic can he learn that it should be pronounced *fizik !*

Reading (says Mr. Parkhurst) should invariably precede spelling. I do not mean that the child should be kept a long time in learning to read before he commences spelling; but that he should never be set to spell a word until he has first become able readily to read it. The reason is, that reading is much easier than spelling, and that a person cannot spell by thinking how a word *sounds*, but he must recollect how it *looks*.

Very many more testimonies might be cited to the same facts. The old system should be uprooted and abandoned, alike in schools and in family instruction, and one more consistent with common sense adopted.

Jacotot has the credit of being the first to introduce one which consists of an abandonment of all alphabetic teaching, making the children begin by pronouncing such words only as are most familiar to them, accustoming them to connect the sound, the sense, and sight. A few sentences should be read slowly and distinctly by the teacher, pointing to each, and simultaneously repeated by the children. After frequent repetitions, they will begin to distinguish the words, and shortly after to point them out in other sentences. The subject of the sentences should present some striking picture to the child's mind, and should be illustrated by wood cuts. The same words should be frequently repeated. Animals, flowers, productions in field or garden, instincts of animals, &c., would be fit topics. Pestalozzi has given numerous examples. The reading lessons should always be preceded by conversational explanations of the subject, so as to lead the child's mind to it and interest him in it, for at no period is it more important that the child's will should be engaged in his work and tedium prevented. All this was generally done in Germany thirty years since, and perhaps it is not premature to expect its adoption here now.

After the child has learnt the *words* in a sentence, he may then be taught the sounds and names of the *letters;**

---

* An addition to this has been suggested by Mrs. Williams, who has published cards for its adoption. Above all the consonants she places a picture, and under it a syllable representing the sound of the consonant, and beginning with it; as, for example, *Butterfly—Bur-bur; Custard—*

but this is of secondary importance, and ought never to precede them.*

It may be objected, that it will be difficult to teach very young children on this system. The best answer is, that it is wrong to teach very young children at all. It is the great mistake to begin education too early. Most assuredly, the child who begins the above recommended system at five years old, will, if his education be consistently pursued, have learned more and retained more at seven, than the child who has been dragged through the old method beginning at four.

HOW TO CURE BAD READING.

Let us proceed to make one or two brief remarks on the best mode of preventing bad reading. The best reading generally follows the best comprehension of the subject, hence the rule, 'read naturally, and you will read well;' for if the reader feels what he reads, he is less likely to do so in a constrained or unnatural tone. Two-thirds of the children in schools do read in this unnatural tone, because they neither know nor care what they are reading about. The two primary rules for making children read well are, first, to make them thoroughly understand what they are reading about; and, secondly, that the teacher should read well to them, making them repeat the same words in the same tone, with the same stops, emphasis, fluency, and

---

Cur-cur; Dunce—Dur-dur; and so on. The vowels are not so well represented; and when the child is more advanced, and sees these letters, it often begins as usual—bur, cur, rur, whether the word is bat, cat, or rat. It is therefore a method which requires a good deal of care in applying.

* There is another system, termed 'the phonic,' which divides the letters into eight classes (!) such as palatals, g (hard), l, k, c, x, q; nasals, m and n; gingcouls (!), d, t, j, &c. It is at once complex and difficult, to say nothing of the total inappropriateness of the names of these classes of letters. Mr. Browne, one of Her Majesty's Inspectors, says it is obvious that 'much care and patience and systematic attention to the classification and gradation of sounds are essential to success;' and for those very sufficient reasons is it wholly unfit for the purpose.

expression. If the teacher cannot do this—and not very many can—neither can his scholars read *well*.

The principle of imitation must be applied negatively as well as affirmatively: the teacher must not only be imitated, but he must himself imitate the faults of his scholars, in order that their ear may appreciate the difference. This should be done with good humour, and so as to give the least possible pain: but without this it will be found impossible to get rid of that inveterate drawl and sing-song accent which infest so many of the country districts.

The Rev. Mr. Bellairs makes the following sensible remarks in his report for 1848-9:—

For good reading, the following should, I think, be insisted on :—

1. A distinct pronunciation of every word.
2. A clear perception of every word; first, when separate, and secondly, when in combination, in order to
3. A correct emphasis.
4. An ocular command over words and sentences, in order to fluent expression.

To express these, I am of opinion that the following plan will prove successful :—

1. The master and scholars to read each word simultaneously.
2. The teacher to explain to the children the meaning of all the difficult words, and to interrogate them thereon.
3. The teacher alone to read to the children each sentence of the lesson as it occurs: the children repeating after him, and, as far as possible, catching his mode of expression.
4. The teacher to call out certain children to read parts of the lesson individually, for which purpose the most imperfect readers may be selected.
5. The class to be broken up into small sections; each section to be under the care of the best reader in it, and to be engaged in reading over alternately, the lesson they have learned as above.

When poor children are once taught to read with tolerable fluency and ease, it is surely inexpedient to bestow much more time on their instruction in the specific art of reading. It is but rarely that they will have to read aloud; and, though to read well is at all times a desirable art, it is with them only very exceptionally an available one; and its acquirement ought not to absorb too much of the limited school time of a working child.

The best ordinary secular reading books are unquestionably those of the Irish Society: they rise in proper gradations, and the lower ones are entirely free from those absurdly long, and, to children, unaccustomed words which are found in so many books designed for them. The addition of questions without answers, at the end of each chapter, would be a great improvement.

The Bible ought never, under any circumstances, to be made a class-book, or used to teach children to read. It is a desecration of God's word, and connects that which should be a privilege and a pleasure with one of the most irksome processes in education.

THE COMPREHENSION OF WORDS

is more important than correct reading; for, unless the child understands the meaning of what he utters, he can only read mechanically, and on the parrot system. The reading lesson should never be deemed complete without the children have been made to understand the full meaning of every word they have uttered. No one would credit how little poor children do commonly understand what they read.

It is not until the child is asked what is meant by such words as persecute, precede, command, guiltless, &c., that it is discovered that he has not the remotest conception of what they mean. Profound ignorance prevails among them as to the meaning of very many words which are used in the most familiar conversation among the middle and upper classes, and occurring in almost every line in the Scriptures. The words *consider, reflect, meditate, conclude, perceive, observe, persecute, appease, velocity, relieve, conceive, vigour, deliberate,* and hosts of others equally simple, are as utterly foreign to the children who have uttered them as if the Greek or Hebrew words had been substituted for them. It cannot well be otherwise. Poor children are almost exclusively Saxon or Celtic; and inasmuch as there has been little or no amalgamation of races since the Conquest in the country districts, they use exclusively Anglo-Saxon or Celtic words in their fireside language; and slight pains are taken in the schools to teach them those of Norman origin. I have several times seen by-standers much astonished, after fairly testing and satisfying themselves of the reality of the child's ignorance of Norman and Roman words. This is, of course, a complete barrier, where it exists, to the instruction of the child. Instead of being educated, he is merely mechanically exercised in a verbal jargon, which imparts but little benefit either to his mind or morals.

The child should also be taught to distinguish the senses of words too often treated as synonymous: *covet* and *desire,* for example; *defer* and *procrastinate; reflection* and *thought; persecute* and *illtreat,* &c. &c.

SPELLING.

Spelling should not be taught as a separate branch of instruction, but always as a collateral to reading and writing. To acquire all the incongruous anomalies in our language, and master the various spellings of the sound, *ain,* or *uff,* for example, and the puzzling precedence of *e g i,* by dint of learning Mavor by heart, is indeed up-hill work. The Welsh children master it with marvellous success, a very large portion of their time being devoted to its acquirement, but it is rare to find English children doing so by means of 'spelling lessons.' They are now generally exploded in good schools. The practice of spelling is identified with reading. First as we have seen in the above-mentioned mode of teaching words before letters. In the more advanced stages spelling is learned in nearly everything that is taught, especially in reading and writing, but more so in the latter. In reading, the eye itself imperceptibly learns spelling, and is at length shocked by an error. But writing is the best mode of teaching to spell. 'What,' says the Rev. Mr. Kennedy,* 'is meant by 'spelling,' belongs rather to 'writing' than 'reading;' and the old plan is therefore correctly being superseded by dictation—*i. e.*, by spelling by the slate instead of by word of mouth. Moreover, dictation includes punctuation, which has hitherto been neglected.'

It is essential, I think, to frame sentences for this purpose. Those taken from a book seldom answer the purpose. One of the most useless publications I ever saw was a little book lately published, containing nothing but ordinary extracts from different books for the purpose of dictation, and without any peculiar difficulties of spelling, so that only half the object could be answered by it, and that equally well from the first book that came to hand. The teacher should frame sentences on purpose; no matter with how little sense or beauty; the object is to exercise the child in spelling correctly and writing fluently. Eight heifers and ewe sheep were chewing the cud beneath the tough boughs of an ancient yew tree in that beautiful field. Or: I rode along the Gloucester Road in the rain, with the bridle-reins on my mare's neck. Or: He fainted and feigned to be ill, but the physician gave him nauseous medicine, and he was fain to recover quickly enough from his malady. Let the

---

* *Minutes of Committee of Council*, 1849, vol. ii.

children be practised in such sentences; write their names at the foot of their slates; and let slight rewards be given to those who can write the whole a certain number of times correctly, and without copying from others.*

There is another mode of teaching spelling, easily adopted when the children are a little practised in it by holding out hands, either in class or gallery. Let the teacher put a word to be spelled; he selects a boy who spells it. Instead of saying right or wrong, he repeats the child's answer and takes a show of hands whether it be so or not. If wrong, another child, who has declared by his hand that it is wrong, is asked to spell it rightly, and again the opinion of the class is taken on the answer. This has been often found to enliven the children and excite an interest in a very dry branch of education.

The copybooks are another means of teaching to spell, but are very seldom so adapted. Instead of trite axioms or long names, why not let copies consist of difficult words to spell, in common use—such as Believe, deceive; prey, pray; skein, chain; petition, passion; ate, mete, meat, meet; rein, reign, rain; though, rough, bough, &c. &c. See also *Suggestive Hints for Secular Instruction*, by the Dean of Hereford. The home exercises on his excellent plan, when produced each morning in the different classes, are submitted to the teacher, and the errors are talked over between the teacher and his children, and subsequently reproduced in their corrected form.

WRITING.

Mulhauser's copies are the best; but when these are thought too expensive, let the teacher rule slanting lines from the top to the bottom of the copybook, in the proper

---

* This should be always punished as a lie, and the children so taught to regard it. If they cannot be prevented in any other way, let them be turned two and two back to back as a disgrace.

inclination for the letters, which is usually not upright enough. It is unwise to keep children too long in large hand; the hand they will find it most useful to write is unquestionably running-hand, and this should be arrived at as soon as possible. The teacher ought to keep up a continual inspection of the copy-books. It is very common among bad and negligent ones to set copies and give themselves no further trouble about the children, except to scold for blunders or blots when the whole is done. This is a pernicious abuse, which should be at once checked wherever it is discovered. Bad spelling frequently leads to its detection, and is also a very injurious result of the master's neglect, inasmuch as the children thus copy their own blunders, until the eye becomes familiarized with them, and so the mistake is perpetuated.

It is good for children not only to copy printed extracts from books, but to write compositions as early as possible.

All writing lessons should be on the parallel disks, so that the children face the master, and he can see their postures, and the motion of the hands and fingers. By this means, as recommended by Mr. Kennedy, one copy on Mr. Richson's plan (sold at Darton's, Holborn) would serve for all. A drawing of a hand holding a pen in a proper position should also be placed before the writers: it assists greatly.

Writing should be taught together with reading, certainly not later. The Central Committee of Education, in one of its papers, says :—

With regard to *writing*, we have known little children write words very well upon slates at four years of age, so that there can be no doubt of their capacity to learn at that age ; and sooner we would not begin. The first lessons should be on the elementary forms; the following comprise all these forms, and each should be written till it is conquered.

These being acquired, their progress in the formation and the joining of letters will be rapid. These letters are quite large enough. It is a mistake to make children stretch their fingers an inch up and down in order to accustom them ultimately to do so a quarter of an inch. People do not ride races in order to learn trotting, or bellow in order to practise articulation. Short words in copies are preferable to long ones.

CIPHERING.

This also should be taught early, as children can be soon made to comprehend the principles of the simple rules, and earlier still to commit the tables to heart, and learn notation; but Dean Dawes lays down this admirable precept, which must not be neglected even in the first steps :— 'ARITHMETIC SHOULD BE MADE AN EXERCISE OF THE MIND, AND NOT MERELY AN APPLICATION OF RULES GOT BY HEART.' Nor can the teacher do better than study and apply all that this writer has laid down for his guidance in his *Hints on Secular Instruction*. 'Take care,' says Mr. Dunn, ' that your pupil never proceeds to a second example in any rule until you are quite sure that he thoroughly understands the first, no matter what time may be consumed upon this introductory effect; he must not be allowed to go on with partial and inaccurate notions of what he is about.' The first duty of the teacher, moreover, consists in extending as much elementary instruction as possible to *every* child in the school. This is by no means the usual system. They are far too prone to push a few children on, in order that they may shine in an examination, and buoy up the rest, who frequently know next to nothing. In this way many a bad school passes for a good one, and this is especially the case with arithmetic. I have found the younger children almost universally backward : there are few things that tend more to habits of providence among the poor than such a knowledge of accounts as may enable them to check their score with the shopkeepers, and otherwise economize their humble finances. This is an obvious means, therefore, of giving the practical benefit of education to the poor, for it would ensure better economy among them: useful arithmetic has, nevertheless, been so grossly neglected, that a small portion only of the boys, and fewer still of the girls, can usually cast accounts, or work the simplest sums in Compound Addition. There is also a practice, in almost all the schools, of putting the children through all four of the simple rules before they are taught Compound Addition, which is very inexpedient. In the first place, the transition is far easier from the one to the other, than from Simple Addition to Multiplication, or to Division. Another recommendation is, that Compound Addition is incomparably more useful than any other rule to poor people, and will be used by them at least a hundred times whilst they want to multiply or divide once. It is essential, therefore, to teach it to as many children as possible before they leave, as shoals of them do now, without being able to cast a figure. Any child of average ability, *if well taught*, may learn to cast simple accounts in four months, knowing nothing but the figures when he begins.

If a teacher wishes to do justice to his school, he will never delegate to another the whole work of teaching arithmetic to any one child. He will so manage as to give some instruction to each. He will himself explain each operation over and over, till it is understood, with the aid of the black board, without which his labour will be doubled; and he will also especially avoid that last resource of laziness—setting children to copy sums for themselves out of arithmetic books, and to work them by themselves. *Every sum should be written down* by himself *from dictation*, or the child will fail to learn half what he ought to learn. It is by neglecting this that so few children comparatively can numerate or notate correctly. I have known many, nominally in Practice or Reduction, who were puzzled to write down such a sum as this:—

£	s.	d.
80,907	0	$0\frac{1}{2}$
8,080	12	$0\frac{3}{4}$
	19	10
100,909	1	$1\frac{1}{4}$

And I may add, that some teachers could not write it either from dictation.

Mental arithmetic should be encouraged, and applied to the solution of practical subjects—the following questions, for example:—What will 4 ounces of tea come to, at 5s. per lb.?—9 articles at 6s. 8d. each?—15 at 16d.?—the poles in $3\frac{1}{2}$ roods?—the difference between 12 square feet and 12 feet square? If 15 loaves cost 2s. 1d., what will 9 cost? How many cubic feet in a cubic yard? &c. Children are but indifferently instructed who cannot readily reckon these mentally, and also state how they work them. The astounding answers sometimes made to questions which seem to require much calculation, but which are really done by a mere trick, should be discouraged. They lead to no good result, and are well calculated to break down a high sense of truthfulness by the sanction they afford to false appearances. The Rev. Mr. Thurtell, Fellow of Caius, and Her Majesty's Inspector of Schools, said on the subject:—

It is to be regretted that exercises in mental calculation should not be employed at every stage of the pupil's progress for developing his conceptions of the relation of number, and rendering his use of arithmetical rules more intelligent. Children may easily be converted into machines for ready reckoning, but, in a practical view this is scarcely worth while, and for the scholar's education, exercises gone through in this spirit are of small service. I was glad to meet with no instance of the tricks by which apparently prodigious results in power and rapidity of calculation are sometimes produced in order to astonish.

Of all mental powers, that of calculation exists in the

most varying measure. Applying, therefore, the great rule I have ventured to lay down, as to the cultivation of the peculiar talent of each child, especially to this branch of instruction, let the teacher carefully select those children who evince the greatest amount of it for the higher rules; carefully excluding from them such children as can, with greater profit to themselves, devote their limited school-time to other subjects.

The first thing, after mastering the first four rules, including their concomitants—viz., Reduction and Proportion, is to drill them well in fractions. This may be simplified. I have found that children best understand what a fraction is by physical illustration, which may be done easily by cutting several sticks of a foot each into a different number of parts, some of them into twelfths, others into fourths, thirds, &c. These are to represent denominators. The numerator will be *named*, and require no such illustration. The most easily understood definition of a fraction is, *that it represents certain equal parts of a single number or thing, the denominator telling the number of parts into which it is divided, and the numerator how many of those parts there are in the fraction; in other words, how many of them the fraction represents.* Having got a distinct notion thus into their heads, proceed to show how to deal with fractions, and first how to multiply them; the scholar will readily understand how if both numerator and denominator be multiplied by the same figure, the fraction is unaltered in value. For example, let the numerator and denominator of $\frac{3}{4}$ be multiplied by 3. It may be shown that $\frac{3\times3}{4\times3} = \frac{9}{12} = \frac{3}{4}$ to ocular demonstration, by cutting another stick of the same length into 12 parts, taking 9 of them, and showing, by placing them together, that they measure exactly the same length as the three-fourths.

Subtraction of fractions may be illustrated similarly, by showing that to find the value of $\frac{3}{4} - \frac{1}{4}$, one of the fourths, or fourth part of the whole, must be taken away, and $\frac{2}{4}$ will remain.   So in the multiplication of fractions: show that by multiplying the numerator we increase the parts taken, or denominators, and that if we wish to multiply $\frac{3}{4}$ by 3, we have to take nine fourth parts instead of three, and we shall, by putting together nine of these fourth parts of the stick, have three times as great a length as before.   Similarly may the division of fractions, by the multiplication of the denominator, be illustrated.   If we thus divide $\frac{3}{4}$ by 3, we now get for our new denominator only the twelfth parts of the stick, and this we find is only a third in length of the fourth parts, and therefore the three-twelfths will be seen to be a third part only of the three-fourths.

The addition of fractions with the same denominator may of course be shown even still more easily.   As regards those with different denominators, it is obvious that the impossibility of adding them as they are, will be well illustrated by the parts of sticks; the one-fourth and the two-thirds, supposing the numerators were added, could not be called either three-fourths or three-thirds, for they would visibly be neither the one nor the other.   What, then, must be done?   How shall we so alter the separate fractions as to make them nevertheless represent the same values, and enable us to add them together ?   To tell the child to multiply each numerator by all the denominators except its own, and all the denominators together for a new denominator, and then to set him to do it, *teaching him nothing more*, is to follow the wretched system of rote learning.   I think the sticks may be used at first to show the facts. Take the fractions $\frac{2}{3}$ $\frac{1}{4}$.   The child having been made to multiply according to the rule, obtains the fractions $\frac{8}{12}$ $\frac{3}{12}$.   Let him take two-thirds of the stick, and place by the side of them eight-twelfths; he will then see that they make equal lengths, and that the rule laid down, namely, to alter the fractions into some others of *like value*, has

been observed.   Similarly with the change of $\frac{1}{4}$ to $\frac{3}{12}$.   Let
him next add the numerators, and give them the common
denominator $= \frac{11}{12}$.   Let him now assure himself, by measurement, that eleven-twelfths of the stick is the same as
two-third parts and one-fourth part of it.   Now explain
the principle.   Recall to the child's mind the former rule,
that by multiplying the numerator and denominator of a
fraction by the same number, you do not alter the value of
that fraction.   If need be, go patiently again over the
proof of that, by reason and with the parts of sticks.   Then
show him that this is just what he has been doing when he
reduced the two fractions to a common denominator.
Taking the first fraction, $\frac{2}{3}$, he multiplied the numerator by
4, and he also afterwards multiplied the two denominators
together, and the other denominator was four.   So that he
did exactly that which does not alter the value of the fraction—namely, he multiplied both of them by 4.   Similarly
in the other fraction, $\frac{1}{4}$, he multiplied both the numerator
and the denominator by 3; and so both the new fractions
were of the exact value of the original ones, but they now
had the same denominator, and this enabled him to add
them.   Proceed then to longer examples, and show that
exactly the same set of facts obtain.   If there be a dozen,
each numerator will be multiplied by eleven denominators,
and by the *same* eleven denominators will its own denominator be multiplied; thus in each fraction will each
numerator and each denominator be multiplied by the
same figure, and its value remain as it was.   We need not
stay to illustrate how similar physical demonstrations may
be applied to the distinction between proper and improper
fractions, and how, to a considerable extent, it is applicable
to algebra.

Dean Dawes, whose steps these remarks have been
humbly following, shows how ocular proof may be given
of solid measures, &c.; nor can there be a doubt that, in

all teaching, we ought to bring everything in its most tangible, practical shape before the child's mind. Education has hitherto been nearly an abstraction; let us strive to reduce it as much as possible to realities.

<hr />

CHAPTER IV.

Higher Branches.

GEOMETRY is by no means a useless branch of instruction for children of the working class.

In the first place, it is useful because it is of all other sciences that which exercises and strengthens the reasoning faculties, and thus improves the power of correct judgment. This is a most valuable boon. Right reason is little else than drawing right conclusions from given facts; and this is the essence of all mathematical science. Its phraseology, moreover, is as precise as its deductions are accurate; so that not only does this study teach us to think justly, but also to express ourselves correctly. This again is a great advantage, for much evil results from defects in each of these points. Endless, and often disastrous, are the evils which arise from false judgment, and almost equally so are misunderstandings caused wholly by the slip-shod way in which imperfectly educated people express, or rather mis-state their meaning. For both these defects, there is no corrective more useful than the first four books of Euclid. In schools, geometry should be demonstrated, as the Dean of Hereford recommends, on the principle of practical application; and, as far as possible, by visible illustrations.

It should be so taught, that it may be applicable especially to carpentering and engineering. One or two examples from *Hints on Secular Instruction,* will illustrate how to do this.

It will be found very useful in fixing on their minds any particular geometrical truth likely to be of use to them afterwards, if the teacher tests it by application to actual measurement, and not to rest satisfied with proving it merely as an abstract truth : for instance, in this schoolroom there is a black line, marked on two adjoining walls, about a foot from the floor ; as the walls are at right angles to each other, of course these lines are also ; they are divided into feet and divisions of a foot, numbered from the corner or right angle, then taking any point in each of these lines and joining them by a string, this forms a right-angled triangle. The boys having learned that the sum of the squares of the two sides containing the right angle is equal to the square on the third side, the teacher will tell them, for instance, to draw a line between the point marked six feet on the one, and eight feet on the other ; square each number, add them together, and extract the square root, which they find to be 10 : then they apply the foot rule, measure the string, and find it is exactly ten feet by measurement.

In teaching them land-measuring, they should be made to understand on what principle it is that they reduce any field complicated in shape to triangles, squares and parallelograms ; why they make their offsets at right angles to the line in which they are measuring; to be able to prove the propositions in *Euclid* as to the areas of these figures, &c., that a triangle is half the parallelogram on the same base and altitude, &c. ; and not do everything mechanically, without ever dreaming of the principles on which these measurements and calculations are made.

The Rev. Mr. Woodbridge, in his *Machinery of Education,* aptly remarks :—

How few in our schools, or among farmers or mechanics, have a clear and distinct idea of what is meant by a cube, or solid inch, or foot, or mile ! And, until a person has a clear conception of that original elementary idea in solids, how can he move one step on the subject, except by groping in midnight darkness ? And how is he to gain a conception of that idea, except by some familiar practical illustration ? Three or four years ago, a gentleman sold a right of some water for carrying a mill. The quantity first agreed upon was a stream which could be discharged through a two-inch tube. When asked what he should charge for the quantity which could pass through a four-inch tube, he answered, 'Twice the price of the other.' The purchaser, of course, obtained four times the water for twice the money, as a tax upon the seller's ignorance; which a glance at a diagram might have removed.

GEOGRAPHY.

Many teachers begin by wandering through the world, and puzzling the children with zones, meridian lines, &c. without any globe to make them intelligible. Many more teach the four quarters, oceans, &c. before they have given the children any definite knowledge what a map is, or even the rudest notion of topography. I would begin at home. Give them an idea of the towns and villages around them on a county map, and instruct them in whatever was most noteworthy about them. I would proceed next to any peculiarity of soil or produce, and also to indicate the hills, mountains, rivers, and all other topographical features. Even this sketch of their own county would be advisably introduced by a rough outline of the village or town in which the school is. Thus I would go, step by step, from the best known to the less known, and so proceed from county to country, from country to continent, and from continent to the world.

The great rule should be, throughout the teaching of geography to children, to make it a series of vivid pictures, and to clothe the skeleton of *names* with the life-like features which characterize places. This is the only way to make geography either pleasing or thoroughly useful to working children. Every kind of fact which tends to give useful or interesting notions of countries or places opens the mind, as well as affords the specific information. Commercial geography is very essential, and all the commercial features of countries, places, and seas or rivers, should be prominently described. Railways ought to be described, and their lines traced. For this purpose, the map in Bradshaw's *Guide* may be used. After tracing the great lines there, it will be a good exercise to trace their course in the large map of England, and show the counties they run through.

English geography ought to be mastered first; and children ought to be able to tell where are Sheffield, Macclesfield, Whitehaven, Penzance, Maidstone, Devonport, and Ipswich, with all their chief features, rivers, &c., before they ever hear of the Ganges or Copenhagen. Until the home land, in which they have to live, and out of which nine hundred and ninety-nine thousandths will never stir, (in truth, this proportion rarely if ever leave their native county,) be pretty well understood, a very slight and general idea of other lands will suffice. This will be probably acquired by seeing the maps of Europe and the world, and being occasionally told what they are, and their main divisions.

A great deal of the physical part of geography may be taught out of doors during walks. As Mr. Dunn says :—

If you wish a child to have correct notions about lakes, islands, or isthmuses, you will be much more likely to insure his possessing them, by referring him to the peculiarities of a neighbouring pond or rivulet, than by any abstract description whatsoever. The *name* of mountain, and valley, and lake, and river, should indeed be invariably connected with the observation of hill and hollow, pond and brook.

Let it be always borne in mind, that physical illustrations are the best modes of teaching, where they are feasible. Thus the raised maps, with the mountains in relief, are useful.

Let the scholars be exercised in drawing maps themselves, which, as a reward for skill, they may be allowed to colour. Let this be done first of the district or county in which they live, marking all the towns and chief villages, &c. Another writer on this subject, says—

It is scarcely necessary to add, that as no description can be equally useful with the view of objects themselves, it is desirable that the pupil should learn the geography of the neighbouring country, as well as his own town, as much as possible from *personal observation*, and be accustomed to describe and delineate its outlines.   It should only be after his own sketches are executed that he should be furnished with more complete engraved maps of the same region.

The principle is no doubt sound, but it is carried here a little too far.   It is not likely that children would be able to draw maps with any approach to correctness before they had carefully examined good ones.   The order should be reversed.

Really good maps are very expensive.   Arrowsmith's are excellent; but for ordinary schools and purposes, the best of the ' Society for Diffusing Useful Knowledge' are sufficient, and they are very cheap.

There should be a map of Palestine and Canaan, of the British Islands, Europe, and the World, and a good county map, in each school.   *County school maps,* I believe, do not exist; but a set, at a reasonable price, on a scale of a third of an inch to a mile, reduced from the Ordnance maps, would be a great boon, if published at a reasonable price.*   The railways should be marked.

Set lessons in geography must be given, but as much as possible should be interspersed in the reading lesson.   If a county or town be ever so casually named in the subject-matter, invariably ask where it is, and have its position indicated, and something told about it, unless it be a place the children are already familiar with.   Such stray shots tell far more effectually than the aggregate lesson, which usually wearies some one in the class unless it be very cleverly given.   Nevertheless, there is nothing which so

---

* Say 5*s.* each for the smaller counties, and 6*s.* or 7*s.* for the larger. Having consulted persons likely to be able to judge correctly, I have no doubt that the sale would far exceed that of the school demand, and that they would be generally purchased.

keenly enlivens and excites as maps. They are the salt of
schools; and the teacher is dull indeed if they do not
savour the other food. I have seen wonders worked with
them in workhouse schools, where we have perhaps the
dullest of dull children to deal with.

It is not so easy as it seems to give a map lesson.
Some make all the children point to a place, when named,
with sticks. A grotesque appearance it has; they usually
wait for the bell-wether of the flock, and then every stick
darts after his; and the thing becomes quite a mechanical
game. The map gets sadly poked and scratched. To ask
individual children to show the places, &c., is a quieter
mode; but this, if carried through the class, is a long
process, and piecemeal work. The teacher must chiefly
handle the map. Let him trace rivers and boundaries,
making mistakes; and create a rivalry, who shall detect
them soonest. This is one way of varying the process.
Let *him* point to places, and the children name them;
making the eldest, as a common rule, remain silent till the
younger have tried to tell. For this purpose the map
must be far removed from the children, or they will read
the answers.

Let especial pains be taken to teach the different industrial districts : the iron districts, the coal districts, the tin,
copper, and lead ; the hardware, cotton, silk, and linen
manufactures ; the pottery, cutlery, &c. &c., with the chief
towns of each. Why are there not industrial maps, as well
as geological, coloured according to industry ? It would
greatly assist the teaching of the ' arts of life,' and be useful
for general information, as well as commercial geography.

It may be as well to say, that of all the things vilely ill
taught in inferior schools, geography is perhaps the worst.
It arises partly from inaptitude and laziness in the teacher,
and from a prejudice against this particular branch of
instruction. It is one of those old English crotchets—

heir-looms of the narrow-minded ignorance of the middle ages—which still make hosts of people, not otherwise bereft of sense, hostile to teaching any geography to poor children. I believe a vast deal of the prejudice centres in the term. It is Greek, and has a learned sound. I wish it could be called by some short Saxon-sounding word, indicating knowledge of places; because, perhaps, it would not seem quite so absurd then to talk of teaching *this* to poor children. It used to be the policy of the poor-law to encourage the poor to migrate from place to place where work could be had; and no one objected then, that to do this effectually the poor ought to have some little knowledge of places; and yet certain good people would have been horrified then, as now, at the bare thought of teaching them geography.* The difference is but verbal notwithstanding.

Maps should always be open on the wall. Children learn a great deal by frequently looking at them. They thus acquire outlines imperceptibly.

There are very few good school-books on geography. That of the Irish Society contains as much as most, and as clearly put as any; but they are all too cut and dry —scraps, rather than descriptive pictures. *Near Home*, is an admirable book, but it is not a school-book. The teacher should buy it, and similar works, and then be the book himself. Hughes's *Geography*, just published, is a useful little book, and so is Sullivan's. *The Earth and Man*, by Guyot, is a book full of useful hints and information for teachers.

---

* An inspector of a workhouse school having recommended maps, they were at length very unwillingly purchased and hung up. Shortly after he was remonstrated with for having had two *globes* for pauper children, which it was affirmed were in the room at his order. Much astonished, he went to the spot, and found that the said globes were the ordinary double map of the World, in the two circular hemispheres, hanging on the wall, which an erudite guardian, in his wrath against 'Jography,' had devoutly believed were globes! This is a literal fact.

HISTORY.

This should be doled out in very small portions to all but very advanced scholars. Its use, at best, has been over-rated. In the first place, we have but dim lights and imperfect knowledge of past times and events. Historians are able, for the most part, to give us only the salient points. The mountains, the dales, the storms, torrents, and volcanoes predominate; and the even tenor and quiet features of the landscape which chiefly composed and characterized it, are lost sight of, so that the whole appears in false colours, and out of its proper perspective. If any one will take up the different histories of no remoter times or personages than Cromwell and Mary of Scotland, he will find them painted in nearly all the shades between a fiend and an angel by different writers, all of them truthful and diligent inquirers,—a proof of the impossibility of learning the exact facts of past times, or even their general aspect. If this be so, can we rely on history as a lesson whereon to draw sound conclusions for the conduct of life? To some extent, we may do it; but little more than we could also draw them from the best works of fiction. This remark applies, of course, to the details of history; its great land-marks are sufficiently authentic, and are easily learned, and it is right to know them; but they avail little towards the culture of the mind, and still less to that of the heart.

History should, for the most part, be introduced like geography, into the reading lesson, and whenever it becomes pertinent to the subject in hand. Set lessons in history are usually confined to the first classes, and rightly so. They then form the ordinary reading lessons of the day, and, if well-selected books be used, this is the best mode of introducing history. The best hitherto have been,

Davy's History of England, and *Hogarth's Outlines;* Mr. Dickens is now publishing a *Child's History of England,* which is more interesting than correct, but much more adapted, in style, to a child's mind, than any other I have seen. Some other writers have recently furnished another new series of little books on English, Colonial, and Sacred History, but certainly not in a style or phrase adapted for young scholars.

It is an evil to condense history or geography. They cease to be interesting; for so voluminous is the matter, and so numerous are the events of importance, that a condensation becomes a string of abrupt facts, much isolated and little readable.

As in geography, so in history, all depends on the use the teacher makes of them, and the living spirit he puts into his instruction. Professor Moseley most truly says, ' that the geography, history, and grammar of the elementary school are mere *fact-teaching*—the teaching of facts from which no conclusions are drawn, and which follow one another in an endless cycle and with a continual repetition. The mind of an intelligent youth famishes, at the age of sixteen or seventeen, on food like this.' Doubtless, and long before then. The number of men who have imbibed a distaste for learning, and remain ignorant for the rest of their lives, because they have been disgusted by this brainless mode of teaching at school, is past belief; in fact, bad schools have been a great cause of ignorance.

History, like geography, is often turned upside down in schools; and children who have not the remotest notion of the distinction between Brunel and Buonaparte, or the Reformation and the French Revolution, are elaborately instructed in the invasion of Britain by Julius Cæsar, and so trudge downwards through the Heptarchy, the Danish and Norman conquests, &c. &c., until, long before they arrive at modern times and useful history, nine-tenths of them leave school, and forget Caractacus and William Rufus with all possible expedition.

It is by no means unusual to find children answering minute questions in the history (as we call it) of times eight hundred years ago, who do not know whether Ireland is governed by England, or what are the chief features of our own Constitution.

School books for children on history might very beneficially begin with a short and plainly written account of our present constitution, including a concise statement of the nature and administration of the law. These subjects appear to me to be quite as important for a poor child to learn as about the battle of Hastings, or the wars of the Roses. The history, chiefly instructive for them, relating to past times, will be that of inventions, manufacture, and commerce.

Sullivan's *Geography and History* is a very useful book for the teacher.

GRAMMAR.

The English grammar should be taught to all boys, but it should be only in its rudiments. Poor children will not need to be learned in syntax. If they know the parts of speech, and how to express themselves with tolerable correctness, it is all that can be required; indeed, only the upper classes can be taught this without detriment to other studies. There are particular parts of the country where attention to this point should be greater than elsewhere. In Yorkshire it will be more needed, for instance, than in Radnorshire, where I believe the English language is both spoken and pronounced more accurately than elsewhere. We shall never break down all provincialisms to the level of pure English; but we may and ought to get rid of the grosser inaccuracies and *patois* dialect which render some of them actually unintelligible. Care should be taken, however, not to uproot old Saxon words, which are often used by the poor and by no other class. These words are sometimes purer and more expressive than the Anglo-Norman terms we have not, very happily, substituted for them.

The Dean of Hereford says, in his *Hints*—

Grammar is taught here (King's Somborne) almost entirely through their reading lessons, and in this way, far from being the dry subject many have supposed it to be, it becomes one in which they take great interest. Any attempt at giving them dry definitions of parts of speech and rules of grammar is almost sure to fail; for one which it interests it will disgust ten, and therefore the thing ought not to be attempted in this way.

The plan is to point out in the reading lessons, first, the articles, where and how to use them, making the children themselves find out examples, and so with the other parts of speech. When a little practised, the teacher should give sentences with bad grammar, and make the children point out the mistakes.

COMPOSITION.

This is a famous mental exercise, and it affords a vast field for instruction in grammar, style, and also in the subject matter of the essay. Some topic with which the children are familiarly acquainted should be selected. Never set them to write formal essays on any of the cardinal virtues or vices; a life of Nelson, or William the Conqueror, or Moses, is less objectionable, but less likely to bring out their minds and interest them, than if they were to write on what they did yesterday: on the work going on in the ground or garden, on some excursion, or on some interesting account they had been reading, of something modern and life-like.

Mr. Bowyer, who inspects workhouse schools, and there has experience in the highest class of education—because the most difficult to accomplish, and applied to the class who need it most—speaks thus of the success of composition exercises, and how to make them useful :—

The point to which I more particularly directed my attention in the past year, was the introduction of composition. Previously there was only one school in which it was practised, and the utmost use to which the art of writing was ever put, was writing from dictation or memory. I have, however, unless the school was so bad as to render it out of the question, invariably made composition an essential part of the inspection; and, even in some instances, its principal medium, by taking the exercises as the subject of oral examinations, and I have found that by adapting the subject to the character of the school, very fair specimens may be obtained, even from those of the humbler description. In an ordinary school, under a mistress, for example, the first class would be able to write a fair abstract of a chapter of the scriptures, consisting of narrative, or a short life of one of the patriarchs; while in a school of the highest class, they would be able to accomplish an abstract of a chapter from the 3rd, 4th, or 5th Dublin Reading Books, or a reign of a king of England. These exercises, excepting the worst, should then be read before the whole class, and should form the text of an examination in a plain 'common sense' way, upon the subject matter, the proper order in which it should be treated, the spelling, the punctuation; and (in the better class of schools) the grammar. If this be done without formality or pedantry, it is a source of much interest and amusement to the children, especially if care be taken to compare the exercises, and point out in what respect one may be better than another. The misspellings, mistakes, confusions, and omissions, which even intelligent children fall into when unaccustomed to express their ideas in writing, thus become an important means of practical instruction, and exercise of the reasoning faculties, and afford an opportunity of bringing into use the rules of grammar, which are otherwise a merely ornamental accomplishment. Writing from dictation or *verbal* memory, on the contrary, which is the utmost attempted in most schools, can only serve as an exercise in spelling, but not in grammar, punctuation, composition, and reasoning.*

---

* *Report on Parochial Union Schools* for 1848-9-50, presented to Parliament by the Committee of Council.

ARTS OF LIFE AND EVERY-DAY KNOWLEDGE.

The reading lessons books of the Irish, and British and Foreign, and the Society for Diffusing Useful Knowledge, contain tolerably well-selected subjects for this purpose. Many of the lessons give practical and useful information on them, but it would be well to have a series which should be exclusively on the useful arts of life—brewing, baking, gardening, carpentering, and on every kind of useful knowledge. One great mistake is, to assume that children know these things already. If classes be thoroughly well questioned and probed, it will be found but very few can give correct or intelligent answers to questions such as these—What is glass made of? What are soap, brass, or lime? If we ask the mode of making them, or their various properties, or where the two former are made, we shall get still less information. Many boys do not know what malt is, or whether it is made from oats, barley, or wheat, still less *how* it is made. The times of sowing and planting, the modes of managing animals and their habits, the culture of the ground, the different kinds of soil, the manures that suit them, the different kinds of timber trees, and the properties and uses of their woods, are all subjects, and many, many more, which seem to me to be useful for working-class boys and girls to know; but how little can we expect to obtain answers about such things, when so many are found ignorant how to plant potatoes, and how long it takes to boil them. The handicrafts, their localities, and the physical and moral features connected with them, wherever they are interesting or useful to know, should be surely taught.

Every teacher who is ignorant of these things, should set to work to learn them: then every walk he takes in the fields with his scholars, as well as every lesson they read, will be the means of instruction to them on all such subjects.

The Dean of Hereford, in his *Hints*, illustrates the ignorance even of people living in the country of every-day knowledge by some amusing and instructive remarks on this head, prefaced by some practical suggestions how to give it :—

There is something extremely pleasing and interesting to children in having their attention called to the habits different in structure, in covering, in manner of feeding, in fact, all possible outward differences, a knowledge of which can be acquired by the eyes and by the hands (seeing and feeling), of the beasts and birds about them; and of this a very strong proof is given in what I have related in connexion with my giving to a class of boys a lesson of the following kind, which was suggested by some observations in a book on Natural History, by the Rev. L. Jenyns, on the difference of the way in which animals with which they are acquainted, rise. How does the cow get up? hind feet or fore feet first? How the sheep? How the deer, &c. ? Some will answer right, some wrong, but all think and are alive to the question. Then pointing out to them that all these animals rise with the hind legs first, and that they belong to the class of ruminating, or cud-chewing animals, and that if it is true that in one, two, three, four, &c. particular cases of animals which chew the cud that they rise in this way, whether it would not be likely to be true in all cases—showing them the way of getting at a general rule, from its being true in a number of individual instances.

Then again : how do the horse, the pig, the dog, &c., rise? Hind feet or fore feet first? Do they ruminate? Have they front teeth in the upper jaw? The teacher would point out how they differ from the ox, the sheep, &c.

Children living in the country are very much alive to this kind of instruction, and I found that several of them in going home from school had observed the animals when rising, and gone out of their way to make them get up; thus bringing to the test of experience what they had been taught, and commencing at this early period habits of observation on things around them, which, in after life, may add much to their happiness, and open out sources of enjoyment to them, to which they have hitherto been strangers.

Happening to mention that some observers of the habits of animals thought that sheep more frequently lie down on the left side than the right, I find that many of them count a flock of sheep, as to the side they are lying on, when they see them lying down in the fold or in the field; and I have no doubt will, in time, have counted such numbers as may balance their opinions one way or the other.

Mr. Jenyns says that he mentioned to a farmer, who had passed all his life among animals belonging to the farm, this difference in the mode of rising in the horse and in the ox—the sheep and the pig—and generally in the cud-chewing and non-cud-chewing animals, but that he, the farmer, was not aware of it; and I recollect myself, many years ago, in college combination room, a conversation arising as to whether a sheep had a double row of teeth in front, similar to the horse (and in the same way the cow), when, strange to say, although every one seemed to know that it was the case with the *horse*, yet not more than one or two were aware that the sheep had not; and so many doubts were started about it, that two young men of the party walked a considerable distance to a field where there were some sheep, and caught one of them in order to examine it.

It is obvious that all this and the whole system of practical teaching would be infinitely furthered by the industrial element.   Let a child be trained to apply what it learns, and to have a hand in the work, so as to realize it, and it will be a great benefit and furtherance to its progress in all kinds of practical education.

In the school-room, as much use as possible should be made of the black board, and of the objects themselves, where feasible.   There is a school called the William's Secular School, in Edinburgh, on the same principle as the Birkbeck Schools in London, where these subjects are well taught.   From an interesting report of it, the following account of the mode pursued may be usefully extracted :—

The object-lessons are also made introductory to physiological and moral science. A bone, a skull, the whole skeleton, an anatomical diagram or preparation, is sometimes made the subject of an object-lesson to the younger children ; and thus they become acquainted with the general structure, and some of the functions of their own bodies, preparatory to entering upon a regular course of physiology.

Rudimentary ideas of their own mental faculties are afforded, by leading them to inquire how they know that an object is brown, or hard, or odorous, &c. ; and thus the organs and functions of the senses and perceptive faculties are made, to a certain extent, familiar to them.

*   *   *   *   *   *   *

The comparison of a natural with an artificial object—a piece of flint, for example, with a piece of glass, or a tree with a table —serves as the basis of elementary instruction on the distinctions between raw materials and manufactured articles, on wealth and its production by labour, on the capital required for its production, on wages, profits, division of labour, interchange, commerce, &c.

Having, in this manner, conveyed to the minds of the children some simple, precise, and accurate notions of the forms and qualities of physical objects, the next aim of the promoters and teachers of the school is, to superadd a systematic knowledge of the structure and functions of the human body, and of the faculties of the mind. Physiology, illustrated by a human skeleton, by casts of the muscular system, and by diagrams representing the blood-vessels, the digestive and respiratory organs, and also the brain, spinal marrow and nerves, are used as the basis of explanations of the structure, modes of action, laws of health, and uses and abuses of the bodily and mental organs. Abstract terms and disquisitions are as much as possible avoided, and objects, facts, relations, and mental states, falling within the observation and consciousness of children, and elucidated by numerous and familiar illustrations, are chiefly relied on.

The success of the instruction in these departments exceeds the most sanguine expectations of the promoters of the school, and shows that God who ordained the human faculties, adapted the remainder of creation to them, with a wisdom and goodness which promise results of unspeakable importance, whenever adequate instruction in natural truth shall be generally and successfully conveyed to the opening faculties of the young.

The best mode of ensuring due attention to these subjects is, to give the children an opportunity of *seeing* as many as possible of all the objects—manufactures, natural wonders, or artistic processes, described. These are far better than *rewards*.

The following books are recommended :—

Useful Arts employed in the Production of Food. With numerous wood-cuts. 2*s*. 6*d*.

Useful Arts employed in the Production of Clothing. With numerous wood-cuts. 2*s*. 6*d*.

Useful Arts employed in the Construction of Dwelling Houses. With numerous wood-cuts. 2*s*. 6*d*.

The Writing-Desk and its Contents, taken as a Text for the

Familiar Illustration of many important Facts in Experimental Science. By Thomas Griffiths, Chemical Lecturer at St. Bartholomew's Hospital. 2*s.*

Roads and Railroads, Tunnels, Bridges, and Canals. One Volume, with upwards of a hundred wood-cuts. 5*s.*

All published by Messrs. Parker and Son.

SOCIAL AND POLITICAL ECONOMY.

Its rudiments, as far as they develop the conditions of well-being, the laws of profit, capital, and wages, should be assuredly taught to the more advanced classes. How otherwise can our labourers be fortified against the anarchical errors contained in the vile publications which Mr. Seymour Tremenheere, in the preface to his able and most useful little work on the principles of political science, says, never were more rife since the old French Revolution. Mr. Senior's four introductory lectures at Oxford, on political economy, should be studied by every teacher. Mr. Senior is, beyond all comparison, the ablest modern writer and most original thinker on this subject, and his works accordingly are the best fitted to inform the minds of teachers. For children, as a class-book, Chambers' *Political Economy, for Use in Schools,* may be advantageously adopted. But the best teaching will be from the head of the teacher.

CHAPTER V.

Religious Education and Moral Training.

RELIGION and morals are naturally combined, and the notion that they are distinct things to be kept apart and taught apart is, to say the least, very mischievous to the due furtherance of both. It is to reduce religion to theology and moral conduct to ethics. Scriptural instruction may indeed be so given; religious education cannot.

In most of the inferior schools Scriptural instruction means simply the mechanical reading of the Bible. Mr. Moseley found this the case in 100 out of 134 of his schools. Whether it was understood in them, need scarcely be asked. For how can a child instinctively understand the Bible without explanation and questioning?

I have now here (he adds) found this constant reading of the Scriptures associated with real Scriptural knowledge, except where, in addition to this, the Scriptures are made the subject of a *special* cause of instruction. It is a result, indeed, to which the learning to read mechanically from the Scriptures does not appear at all to contribute, but the reverse. Ideas of the same class, presented incessantly to the mind under the same circumstances, lose at length their interest; and the repetition of them, instead of strengthening the impression they have, tends (a certain limit being passed) to confuse it.

Nor is this the case only with the mere unexplained reading of the Scriptures: it is much the same when they are explained, but where the knowledge so imparted is of abstract truths, and where it is *never put to practice.* Religion is not a mere code of rules and revelation of facts; it has a living spirit; and that spirit can neither be fully felt nor conveyed apart from action. Religion is a thing of life; without which faith itself is dead. We may no more separate them in the seed than in the fruit,—in the school than in the after world. It is the system of schools to do so nevertheless: religion is taught in them just as astronomy or logic, as an abstruse science or a string of truths. The result of this untoward severance of the ethical and practical from the spiritual province of religion, is that each is shorn of the vitalizing power indispensable to their proper culture. The genial relation between God and man—between religion and nature is unseen. The link is wanting, nor can the child supply it. The kingdoms of nature and grace are to him utterly dissevered. The function of Christianity being not only to teach religion to the mind, but to guide and train the native energies of the soul, that system

of education, however biblical its teaching, which stops at
the school door, has done but little for the religious discipline of the heart, and nothing for the practical fruition of
its own code.   Religion is regarded by children thus taught,
as an abstraction full of law and mystical solemnity, wrap-
ped up in a shibboleth of terms and phrases which impart
to their minds vague ideas and no realities.

They do not know, for they have never been trained to feel,
that there is a religion, *in little*, in every part of life: that it
inspires and animates all that is useful, as well as all that is
great and good and virtuous and ennobling.   It is very common to find children who have a perfect knowledge of, at
least, the cardinal means of salvation, and all the leading
truths and doctrines of Scripture, and yet who turn out dis-
solute and depraved, and very frequently worse than those
who have been left in ignorance.

In the first place, the mode in which the teaching
is given and the questions are put is not sufficiently
searching.   The wretched rote system is a great stumbling
block to all comprehension and all mind-work.   To be able
to repeat the Church catechism, or indeed any catechism, is
absolutely nothing.   It no more informs the mind than it
affects the body. Scarcely one out of fifty children who repeat
it are made *thoroughly* to comprehend it.   And yet it contains an epitome of the whole scheme of salvation and the
entire code of moral conduct.   Dissenters frequently ac-
knowledge the extreme merit of this composition as a
whole, one or two doctrinal passages excepted.   The clergy,
who are the mainspring of existing schools, insist almost
everywhere on its use, and yet, strange to say, so little is
it comprehended by the children, that in a great majority
of cases it might as well not be learned at all.   It is impossible to insist too strongly on the necessity for constant
and zealous teaching of its full meaning.

If the epitome be thus neglected, it were vain to expect

the Holy Scriptures at large, in such schools, to be better understood. A system of teaching the Scripture more in unison with the views above stated would, I humbly incline to think, be more effectual. Though, during school instruction in them, there would be no means of applying the doctrines of Scripture to practice, the teaching itself might be made more practical and less dogmatical than it usually is.

The best routine is probably that of (after prayer) reading the portion of Scripture selected distinctly and reverently, taking care not to make it a reading lesson, but simply correcting errors if made. The next step would probably be that of questioning on and explaining the meaning of any words which may require it, so that the sense shall be fully understood. The master should then himself give an explanatory comment on the whole passage; it should be full and yet terse, not overloaded with matter; and yet every difficulty should be explained, and the full effect and bearing of each part be not only pointed out, but *illustrated* by such facts and practical cases as may be most likely to attract the interest and fix themselves, and the truths they exemplify, in the minds of the children. In this branch of the work there is ample opportunity for practical application, and the whole may conclude with brief and earnest exhortation. It is in this action that the whole mental and moral power, as well as the religious zeal and knowledge of the teacher will come into full action. No rules can give him the skill, spirit, and animation which the subject demands.

When this lecture is concluded, and it should never exceed twenty minutes, and seldom seventeen; the children should be left to read over the whole passage to themselves and silently reflect on it. Perhaps twenty minutes may be thus occupied. It depends on the length of the passage and the amount of difficulty and matter for reflection it contains. Whilst this is going on the teacher will be engaged in the quiet superintendence of one of the other divisions—*ex. gr.*, examining copy-books, and correcting errors, &c. Thus he will obtain an interval of repose for mind and voice. He then returns to the Scripture class and thoroughly examines it in the whole lesson, according to the system already pointed out in the chapter on 'How to teach,' both by questioning and holding out of hands, and elliptical explanations when required.

The object of the teacher should be to *lead* as much and to drive as little as possible. Every effort must be exerted to make the children *think*, by putting to and also by drawing from them suggestions of facts, such as may lead to a fuller development of the subject. To obtain questions *from them* is a great object. Habits of investigation may be thus formed and turned into wholesome channels, which will benefit the child to his life's end and beyond it.

It is impossible to dictate rules for questions on this all important subject; it is, in fact, teaching in another shape. The question should be such, however, as relates chiefly to practice. Instead, for instance, of asking what is the commandment against coveting? the question may be put thus: Suppose a boy wishes for something that does not belong to him and thinks no more of it, would he break any commandment? If the children know the difference between coveting and wishing for a thing, they will say 'no.' But suppose he sets his heart on it and keeps on longing for it? Answer: The tenth. Suppose a boy tells a lie about another boy, and says he saw him steal something in order to get him punished, which would he break then? *The ninth.* Suppose he gets into a passion and calls bad names? *The sixth.* Why, and how do we know that? The spirit of the commandments and their extended meaning, as given in the sermon on the mount, will form the subject of useful remarks. Each great doctrine and duty may be made the subject of practical illustration.

The doctrine of atonement may be illustrated by the various modes in which men can make amends to men for wrongs done by them. God only can make amends to God, and hence a divine atonement in the blood of the Saviour was required.

It is of little use (says Mr. Stowe) merely to tell a child not to sin. If you wish to train him not to sin—not to steal, for example, illustrate by such occurrences as Achan in the camp—not to tell lies, by the sad fate of Ananias and Sapphira—not to indulge in pride and vanity by poor Absalom; and when these and many others are fully and progressively pictured out and analyzed the children will be quite prepared to know, and in some measure to feel the principle, ' Be sure your sin will find you out.'

The parables and precepts of our Lord will assist the practical illustration of the moral duties.* The words, 'forgive us our trespasses as we forgive them that trespass against us,' will give occasion to ask what duty is thereby enjoined, and the parable of the unjust servant illustrates it. Some will answer, the good Samaritan. This will open some useful questions on that parable, and also on our Saviour's interview with the woman of Samaria at Jacob's well, who told him ' the Jews have no dealings with the Samaritans.' Instances and circumstances likely to occur among the children should always be used. Supposing Tom Smith did so and so, what ought you to do? Why so and so. Such cases are the most striking examples which can be given to children, and are worth volumes of formal exposition.

Every lesson (as the Rev. Mr. Bellairs judiciously remarks) should be attentively studied by the Master so far as he might glean information thereon before he proceeded to instruct the children on it. By this means he would be able to bring forward such information—historical, geographical, and etymological, as

---

* Scripture proofs and precepts, with references to the parables and commandments, will be found in Appendix C.

would awaken the intelligence of the children, teach them to think, and supply them with intellectual food. From a want of information springs a poverty and inability of interrogation, a defect very apparent in many schools. A common method of interrogating the children is by means of a book of questions. From these the children are interrogated on the lesson in which they are engaged, and no further explanation or inquiry is attempted; if they answer in strict accordance with the words of the book, it is considered that they know all that is needful; frequently no other answer, however correct it be in sense, is accepted, and this work of interrogation, as it is termed, becomes in a short time, on the part of the children, a mere effort of memory but no exercise of the understanding. If the master is conversant with his subject, he will require no book of questions from which to interrogate his scholars.

Mr. Kennedy also admirably remarks:—'It is only active, ever-improving, energetic, living minds, which are fit to instruct and form the minds of others.' Their education has not been of the kind which leads them to be themselves ever learning and thinking, and consequently their minds stagnate.

One of the chief means of giving a knowledge of Scripture, and a lively faith, is to unite with it a thoroughly efficient *secular* education. It is, I believe, the unanimous opinion of her Majesty's Inspectors of Schools, that 'sound knowledge in secular learning and in religion go hand in hand.'* There are not only thousands of illustrations and references in the Holy Scriptures which are inexplicable to a person who has no secular knowledge, but the intellect and the apprehension are sharpened, together with all the mental faculties, by it, and by that world-knowledge, *welt-kunde*, as the Germans call it, which God intended man to know. This is written on every page of nature, and just as clearly on that of revelation.

---

* *Minutes of Council*, 1844, vol. ii., p. 233.

MORAL TRAINING.

Moral training of a practical kind is exceedingly difficult to apply in a school-room, and it can only be done to a very limited extent; and yet, without it, what are we doing for the improvement of the heart and conduct of the child? Next to nothing. Stowe well says :—' Remember that mere Christian knowledge in the head does not morally elevate—practical knowledge alone morally elevates. *Doing*, in conjunction with the understanding and affections, is moral training.' So true is it, that ' knowledge puffeth up, but charity *buildeth up*.'*

It is difficult to understand the ground on which people expect that the ordinary run of schools will moralize the poor. Why should they? Morals are not trained in them: and surely mere reading, even if it be in the Bible, with a complement of writing and arithmetic, has no such tendency. The Rev. Mr. Moseley, though he entertains, perhaps, a less unfavourable view of the effect of the prevalent instruction in schools, says :—

Notwithstanding the favourable view which I have thus been led to take of the progress of religious instruction in our schools, there are some elements in which it appears to me to be deficient. I have found in it, for instance, nothing to represent those admonitions which a religious parent is accustomed to address to his children, with a personal application to the conscience of each, and an individual knowledge of its necessities; and which, appealing to the heart and the affections, have an influence with children greater than that which they yield to reason or to authority. I have moreover, thought, that in the exclusive direction to religious objects which the teaching in some schools receives, the exercise of that discretion was wanting, by which a pious and judicious parent would provide, in respect to the education of his own children, that due care should be taken to encourage a veneration for the Scriptures, and impress them with a due sense of their importance; and that, of all the subjects in which they are instructed, religion should be made the least burdensome to them.

---

* Edifieth is a mistranslation.

Miss Carpenter, in her very interesting and able work on 'Reformatory Schools,' after citing some startling instances of the inefficacy of mere school reading of the Bible, says :—' It is not sufficient to found schools to communicate knowledge, or even to impart religious ' wordiness,' as it is aptly called, without wisdom to direct, and power to guide and control these wild beings. These children were absolutely in a worse condition, one far more dangerous to society, than if they had been left alone to their own ignorance.'

Miss Carpenter says, that ' in too many schools, the Scriptures are made an ordinary reading lesson ;—fami- liarity with the words, without attaching any interesting meaning to the sense, only deadens the heart to the holy truths contained in them, and is a great hindrance rather than help to subsequent benefit being derived from the Scriptures.   Nor even is a full acquaintance with the Bible, and understanding the meaning of it, sufficient to influence the heart and conduct.'—' The most thoroughly unprincipled and unimpressible boy I ever taught in the ragged school,' says the same teacher, ' was one who had long been taught in a Church of England Sunday school, and was thoroughly acquainted with all the facts of Scrip- ture, together with various points of theology, which he would willingly have discussed, had I permitted him.   He gloried in having been mentioned in the newspaper as the head of a gang of thieves, and is now in prison.   Several boys have come to my class for a few times on leaving jail, and I have been quite astonished at the full and accurate Scripture knowledge they have acquired while there ; but in only one or two cases out of many has any permanent good effect seemed to arise from this.   They had read the Bible only, as a Catholic boy said, ' to pass away the time ;' and it had not entered their hearts.'

But should such experience discourage us, or make us

doubt the value of that " Holy Scripture, which is able to make us wise unto salvation ?" Shall we no longer believe the pearl to be of great price to these children, because they cannot discern its lustre and feel its beauty when presented to them under a hard covering of words, to them without meaning, their own eyes being dim with ignorance, and a veil being over their hearts ? Let us rather, believing, as we do, that religion is essential to all reformation, strive to find out how it may be so communicated as really to engage the affections, and influence the conduct. A few suggestions, founded on experience, may be useful.

With those who are totally ignorant and uninformed, formal religious lessons will seldom be advisable; though, as the school improves, they may be made most interesting in regular religious instruction. Reliance must not, however, be placed in these alone ; but the teacher whose heart is thoroughly awakened to the importance of this work, will be ready to seize every opportunity presented by passing events, or the ordinary teaching, of impressing on the child's heart some valuable lesson. The affections must be roused, and a love of virtue and holiness excited. The mere presence of goodness in others has a tendency to soften and purify the most obdurate, on whom its spirit is exercised.

Miss Carpenter also remarks, that religious instruction almost necessarily includes moral teaching ; yet with a class possessing as yet so little distinct notion of right, direct moral instruction, as well as training, must be made a distinct and frequent subject of lessons. It has been remarked by one well qualified to judge by his high legal position, and by his long acquaintance with the juvenile nature, that a large proportion of young criminals are absolutely unacquainted with the " science of morals."

Rewards and Punishments.—These are an essential

part of moral training; but so admirably have the rules for it been laid down by Mr. Stowe, that I should be doing gross injustice to the subject were I to prefer my own views or statements to his. I have only to say, that in this, as in all other branches of moral training, he will find the application of his rules infinitely facilitated by out-door labour.

The understanding of the punishment must be present, or the mere sensation of bodily pain is no punishment to him. Instead, therefore, of passing into the understanding, through the physical department of the human being, we prefer punishing as well as stimulating the higher sensibilities of our moral nature.

If a mother can make it an honour and a privilege to her child to lift her handkerchief, and a punishment not to be permitted to do so; or, if it be possible and practicable that for disobedience or any other fault, a child's exclusion from table for half an hour, is felt to be a punishment so severe, as almost to tear his heart-strings asunder; then it is clear, that by the same process, and by the additional power of sympathy of numbers, which the mother cannot have, may the master of a training school punish a child most severely, without corporal infliction; and so it is in a properly conducted training school, and with a regularly trained master. To order a boy out from the gallery, after being properly warned once or twice, is found to be really more severe than half-a-dozen ' palmies.'

*   *   *   *   *

Corporal punishment in school tends to harden or break the spirit. We ought never to associate the idea of punishment with what we should love. A child ought to love school, and his teacher, and his exercises. To punish a child by causing him to commit a large task to memory, or write a large exercise, or read six chapters of the Bible, is the most certain mode of generating a dislike for all of these. Our object is to stimulate from a fear of offending, rather than from a fear of the rod. Nothing can be more unjust than to punish a boy for a deficiency in the power of calculation, or the memory of words, while he may possess in a high degree reason and imagination—thus stimulating the lower at the expense of the higher powers of the mind.

*   *   *   *   *

The evil principle or practice is pictured out according to the peculiar mode of the system, so that it is seldom necessary to bring out or even notice the individual—the finer feelings of nature have been brought into play—and the downcast look discovers how fully the child feels himself condemned by his fellows and by his own conscience.

*　　　*　　　*　　　*　　　*

Old teachers, and impatient young men, who have been accustomed to use the literal rod to save time, or the trouble of investigating a fault, are apt to imagine that there are difficulties in refraining from the use of it which do not exist. Patience in this department of moral training is indeed 'a virtue,' and lies at the root of all training. From long experience we know, that in exact proportion as a schoolmaster trains, does the use of the literal rod appear to him unnecessary.

Offences of any moment may be dealt with by trial; the children, or some five or six elected by themselves, sitting as a jury, and the teacher as judge. These trials may be made to form excellent practical moral lessons, and aid in bringing home to the minds of the children sound moral rules of judgment. They who pronounce judgment, moreover, on moral offences, are less liable to commit them themselves. They thus learn if the judge does his duty, the reasons of moral laws, and obey them the better for understanding and appreciating them.

Every event in the school should be invariably turned to a moral account—every ebullition of temper, all deviation from truth, honesty, or modesty. All merits, on the contrary, should be noted, if not publicly praised. It is of great importance that children should feel that their good efforts are appreciated. The skilful teacher will know how to do this without exciting vanity, or puffing up the object of his praise. Let him also make it a rule scrupulously to give the fullest meed of it, consistent with truth, to the children he likes least, and to those who are generally the least deserving, and whom he is often obliged to censure. Its effect will be sometimes infinitely greater than any corrective, when faults occur.

Above all things, the teacher should make his scholars love him; it is as powerful an instrument for moral training as it is for good discipline; and this is infinitely better enforced by affection than by fear.

Mr. Stowe long ago discovered that so little does the natural disposition of the child develop itself in the school-room, that he must set the teacher to watch it in the playground, in order to make moral training possible. It can be to a great extent so accomplished; but would it not be a great improvement to substitute some useful work for profitless play? The boy who is digging or planting is surely better employed than he who is twisting himself over parallel bars, or swinging himself round a pole. The body is just as healthily exercised, and, in addition, the boy is receiving most valuable information—feels himself to be useful, and enjoys such employment tenfold more than circular swings or parallel bars.

It is in the various developments of character, and calls for exertion of all kinds of faculties and feelings occurring in out-door labour, that the moral trainer derives his most fruitful and valued opportunities of correcting what is wrong, and encouraging what is right.

Vehrli's remark is wonderfully true, that—

There is no knowledge in books like an immediate converse with nature, and those that dig the soil have nearest communion with her.

Vehrli had good reason to make this assertion, having done wonders by means of spade labour in the education of boys. Although he may properly be regarded some-what as an enthusiast, his long experience, earnestness, and purity of purpose must entitle his opinions to the utmost respect, and some degree of weight, even were his experiences and conclusions not fortified and confirmed as they have been by repeated experiments of a like nature in this and other countries.

Sir J. K. Shuttleworth and Mr. E. Carlton Tufnell, made an educational tour in the year 1840, in the course of which they visited Switzerland and several other countries. In their very able report to the Poor Law Commissioners, published in the *Minutes of Council*, 1842-3, they thus describe the system which formed the basis of the schools of industry instituted in the canton of Berne, at Hofwyl, by De Fellenberg, and which forms an excellent summary of the principles on which the recommendations I venture to make on this head are founded :—

Those orphan and normal schools of Switzerland, which have paid the deference due to the lessons of Pestalozzi and De Fellenberg, are remarkable for the gentleness and simplicity of the intercourse between the scholar and his master. The formation of character is always kept in mind as the great aim of education. The intelligence is enlightened, in order that it may inform the conscience, and that the conscience, looking forth through this intelligence, may behold a wider sphere of duty, and have at its command a greater capacity for action. The capacity for action is determined by the cultivation of habits appropriate to the duties of the station which the child must occupy.

Among the labouring class no habit is more essential to virtuous conduct than that of steady and persevering labour. Manual skill connects the intelligence with the brute force with which we are endued. The instruction in elementary schools should be conducted as not only to assist the labourer in acquiring mechanical dexterity, but in bringing his intelligence to aid the labours of his hands, whether by a knowledge of the principles of form or numbers, or of the properties of natural objects, and the nature of the phenomena by which his labours are likely to be affected. In a commercial country it is pre-eminently important to give him such an acquaintance with geography as may stimulate enterprize at home, or may tend to swell the stream of colonization, which is daily extending the dominion of British commerce and civilization. Labour, which brings the sweat upon the brows, requires relaxation, and the child should, therefore, learn to repose from toil among innocent enjoyments, and to avoid those vicious indulgences which waste the labourer's strength, rob his house of comfort, and must sooner or later be the source of sorrow. There is a dignity in the lot of man in every sphere, if it be not cast away. The honour and the joy of successful toil should fill the labourer's songs in his hour of repose. From religion man learns that all the artificial distinctions of society are as nothing before that God who searcheth the heart. Religion therefore raises the labourer to the highest dignity of human existence, the knowledge of the will and the enjoyment of the favour of God.

Instructed by religion, the labourer knows how in daily toil he fulfils the duties and satisfies the moral and natural necessities of his existence, while the outward garb of mortality is gradually wearing off, and the spirit preparing for emancipation.

I have only one rule to add : The teacher must be what he wishes to make the children. The moral temperament of a school will depend as closely on that of the teacher as will its physical aspect ; and I have seen many wonderful proofs of the change effected in the temper, and in the outward aspect of children, by the change of a morose gloomy teacher for a lively and cheerful one. The deceitful or ill-natured teacher is just as little fitted to make his scholars truthful or good-tempered, as a ploughman is to make lace.

There are many good elementary books on Scripture history, and religious knowledge. No teacher should be without Nicholl's *Guide to the Study of the Scriptures*, or *Outlines of Sacred History*. The Irish *Scripture Lesson Book* cannot be recommended to Protestant schools. It is much to be wished that a work on precisely the same excellent plan were compiled for them from the authorized version. *Line upon Line*, though dear, is a capital book for children.

CHAPTER VI.

School Teachers.

IT would be very beneficial to the future progress of Education if young men and women, and still more if men and women at advanced periods of life would, before adopting the vocation of school teacher, honestly consider whether they have natural abilities for this most difficult and arduous work. It is to be feared that few, comparatively, do it. There is one class who wish to follow it, because they are disqualified from following any other. It were well if such persons could be divested of the delusion that in such case they are any fitter for school teachers. It is an office requiring health and strength,—a clear head, a good heart (humanly speaking), a firm, and above all a kind disposition, a vigorous spirit, great mental energy, liveliness of character, and perfect command of temper. No one of these qualifications can be properly absent in the good school teacher. Now, it is very difficult to understand how a person possessing these qualities should be unable to succeed in any other vocation in life. I should say that the man or woman qualified to fill the high office of school teacher is, on the contrary, likely to be qualified *for almost anything* ; and they who are thus qualified, will alone do for school teachers ; an office which it is not only difficult to fill, but as important as any which a human being can aspire to.

Talkers and writers who are fond of bewailing the shortcomings of society in this country, are wont to cite a great variety of our faults and foibles, blunders and abuses, but strangely they seldom, if ever, hit on the immeasurable mischievousness and folly of our low estimate of teachers. All classes, from the dame school-mistress up to the most highly salaried governesses and tutors, fall under this ban. It is a great mistake. They are moulding for us the character of the generations among which we and our children are to live, and by which our highest interests here must be determined. What is the importance of the functions of the mere law-maker, for example, in comparison to this; if we contrast, as we ought to do, the relative power each wields in determining the destiny, moral and social, of the community? The first thing is for society to retrieve its error in this false estimate. It should be done first by an entire change in the social position of small teachers. They should be placed in another phase, both by sympathy and deference. Those whose rank and moral and intellectual superiority gives them the power of bringing this change to pass, should take means to do it. These means need not be suggested. It is no more than what such superiority owes to itself to have the will, and find the way. Children, and all persons in inferior positions, should be taught to honour teachers: and they will be best taught to do so *by example*.

There is another way in which the same object may be furthered—by a largely-increased liberality in the salaries of school teachers. The standard of payment should rise with that of the esteem in which the office is held. No labourer is better, if so well, worthy of his hire as the school teacher. Let us give it to him liberally. Largely-increased grants from the State are among the means; but where private benevolence can afford them, it is a shame in it to seek public aid; for there can be no higher or worthier object of benevolent effort.

There are now several normal schools of the utmost value for the training of teachers. These institutions cannot be too largely supported. Many more are wanted. All have their merits, but that of Kneller Hall, where systematic industrial labour, combined with excellent instruction, presents all the advantages in unison with the views of education taken in this little book, is a model.

In all such establishments, admirable as their system of training and teaching teachers may be, it is still to be wished that more pains were taken to deter thoroughly unfitted persons from devoting themselves to the office. The principals of these institutions may very easily, and most likely do very quickly, perceive who are and who are not qualified by nature for the work. The idea of rendering them so by art alone is worse than hopeless.

Schools are numerous where the children are now sacrificed to the folly of supposing that because a man or woman has attained a certain amount of knowledge, that they can therefore teach or train children. The letting loose of these people on our schools is a great injury, and it should be prevented by all who have the power, and assuredly none have more than the Principals of Normal Schools, unless it be the parochial clergy, who often suggest this vocation to the persons who adopt it. One great point to be observed is, *are they fond of children, and do they like teaching?* If not, let them never hope to succeed.

It is not the proper province of this little work to say more on the mode of training school teachers than is expressed or implied in what has been suggested under the heads of what they are expected to teach. To fit them for doing so is the province of the normal school. Those who cannot avail themselves of such an obvious advantage, should endeavour to obtain admission into some good school, and *see how to teach,* and try their hands. They will thus learn more than by a year's reading at home, or by any amount of oral instruction.

One word as to the choice of teachers. It involves a great responsibility.

It is a common mistake, to appoint them, or to keep them on, *out of charity.* Let the good people who do this, reflect for one moment on the injustice done to the many children put under the charge of an incompetent teacher. Are they not of infinitely more concern? and is it not a bitter injustice done to them, for the sake of a single individual, thus undeservedly pensioned, at the sacrifice of their highest interests?

PART THE THIRD.

INDUSTRIAL TRAINING.

CHAPTER I.

Field Gardening for Schools, with Supplementary Employment in other Handicrafts.

SPADE husbandry is generally admitted to be the best, though it is by no means the only, sort of industrial labour which is applicable to the case, and annexable to schools; and this chapter will be devoted to the development of that which will usually be found the most useful system—namely, the cultivation of ground on the most approved system of field gardening, with a junction of some one or two handicraft employments.

'Field-gardening' is a term applied by Mr. Nowell in his useful manual on the subject.* It means the adaptation of the spade, fork, rake, hoe, and dibbler, to the cultivation of fields, and also those minuter and more careful attentions to manuring, planting, weeding, birdscaring, &c., which are always devoted to gardens.

We at once see how applicable this is to boy labour. Most of these minute operations require manipulations and incessant bending, which the active fingers and lower stature of boys enable them to perform far more easily than men can do it. Even in digging and the other work to be done,

---

* Published by Simpkin and Co., price 2s.

the same result is found; and though, of course, allowance is to be made for different strength, the boys work nearly as well, and more continuously, than men. They enjoy it, and stick to it much more steadily.*

Many persons, well-disposed to annex industrial training to their schools, will doubtless be deterred by the fear of its impracticability in their own locality; and there are, doubtless, schools where any sort of garden or field labour would be so, and for the present we must defer the consideration of such cases. In the vast majority of country schools, and in many of those situated at the outskirts of towns, it is generally quite practicable, for there, more or less land may always be had. A mere garden is better than none. Do not let the impracticability be too readily assumed.

Let us first consider what would be the most advisable system for organizing industrial field labour where the facilities existed in obtaining ground, and where the promoters were willing to give full effect to the system. We will afterwards descend to the cases in which a more limited adoption of it would be alone feasible.

Ground should be obtained, if possible, adjacent to the school. If this be impossible, it may be taken at a short distance. The distance is, however, in all cases a disadvantage. The children have to go there and back; this is a loss of time, and often prevents their going, and work being done at all, on rainy days. It is almost fatal to the excellent plan of keeping pigs or cows. It may be done still, but under many disadvantages. The last and worst drawback is, that the liquid manure has either to be conveyed to the land, or is lost; whilst there is also the

---

* See evidences in the letters in Appendix D. I have also some boys taken from workhouses who live and work here, and speak from my own experience also.

carriage to the school of all the produce to be consumed there.

The rent given for the land is not of much moment ; the system of cultivation recommended will amply compensate for a very high rent. With judicious management, however, and any approach to liberality on the part of the owners, this drawback, such as it is, may generally be obviated, and the land obtained at a moderate rate.

The quantity taken must depend on the number of boys who can work it. It is not advisable to have more than can be conveniently cultivated by the staff that can be reckoned on. As nearly as I can reduce the experience I have drawn from several establishments where the boys are thus employed, I think the following scale will prove nearly right :—

Number of Boys.	Acres of Digging Ground.		Meadow.	
	a.	r.	a.	r.
5	1		1	
7	1	2	1	
9	2		1	2
12	3		2	
16	4		2	
22	6		2	2

The boys are supposed to vary in age from nine to fifteen years, averaging twelve. If they are materially older or younger, there must be an allowance made in proportion. It is also assumed in this estimate that the schoolmaster works hard with the boys. He must be, coat off, and at it along with them. No fine gentleman schoolmaster is to be tolerated in any school for the education of working boys. If a man is above putting his hand to the spade, he may be fit for a dancing master, or a man milliner, or many lady-like occupations, but assuredly he is not the stuff out of which a schoolmaster, in these times, is to be made, if education means the training of a future generation of hard-working men and women. There must be no puppyism about the teachers of such a race. A capital nursery for really good teachers is that of workhouse schools; and had we but *district* industrial schools for these poor children, apart from workhouse contamination, instead of bringing them up as paupers, such schools would train for us an excellent race of teachers. Some of the workhouse schools are industrial already, and afford, in many respects, excellent examples of spade labour, and of useful household work for girls. In these schools three hours, at least, daily are set apart for school instruction, and a large portion of the rest of the day to labour.

In ordinary schools three and a half or four hours will perhaps not be too much for school instruction; but assuredly it never should exceed that period. This will alone be a great gain over the old system of keeping children at school for six or seven hours. It is a mistake to do so; the attention cannot be profitably sustained for so long a time. On the contrary, when the child's mind is relieved and enlivened, and his bodily vigour increased by labour, he applies with zeal and power to mental work, not sufficiently prolonged to weary him. It has been proved that by this system he learns far more effectually than by the old fashion of exclusive school-work for a greater number of hours. The Quatt School can bear ample testimony to this fact, and to the superior attainments as well as mental activity of the boys educated and worked there, when compared with others schooled, and not worked, in other establishments. Again, it has been noted in the same school, between children who do work and those who do not, with like results. The mental faculties of the former were always the most vigorous and fruitful. The agency takes place not merely by means of bodily energy, which invariably extends itself to the intellect, but the child acquires new ideas, and his mind itself is, directly as well as indirectly, stored and enlarged.

If out door labour is adopted, it will be generally best that the schooling should be in the afternoon. The morning is the best time for labour, and after dinner for repose; and even if it were not, the plan here recommended will render it almost necessary that this should be done.

We have already seen that it will not do to exact labour from the children without giving them some share in its profit. It is proposed to give them their dinner.* It should consist of a small portion of meat, bacon, or soup, alternately; and plenty of bread and vegetables, with water. This meal, of course, is supplied to the boys only who have worked for the allotted hours *during the morning.*

This will not interfere with the payment of the children's pence. If possible, some of the girls should be employed in cooking the dinner, and take their share accordingly in eating it. It will be seen presently how the expense is provided for. The great advantage of this over every other plan is, that the working children will spend their whole day at the school, and be thus more under the continuous influence of the moral training, and be kept from the perilous influence which beset too many of them at their homes and on their way backward and forward. The orderly meal with its short graces, is another instrument for the teaching of decent habits. These are all helps in the work of moral training, which no one will slight who knows what it is.

The best arrangement as to teachers will be this. There must be a master and mistress. The chief work of the master will be the management of the industrial department, with its continuous moral training, and next to this the mental instruction of the whole school in the afternoon. In this the school mistress will assist, and in the morning

---

* Ragged Industrial Schools are established at Edmonton on this principle, after much deliberation. They are scarcely yet in operation.

it is proposed that she should employ the girls chiefly in needlework and superintending the cooking department and washing; those too young for it will be learning to read and write under the eye of the schoolmistress, but taught by a pupil teacher.

NEEDLEWORK*

Is most essential for girls; but by needlework we do not mean making a variety of samplers or using the crochet needle or worsted work, but plain work, such as hemming, sewing, stitching herring-bone, &c. &c., all which are highly necessary for, and should be taught to all girls, but especially to the poorer classes; as what can be a greater drawback to the comfort and economy of a poor family than to have to employ and pay some one to mend and make their clothes; and yet this is constantly done. All girls should begin to learn at five years of age to hem; they should begin on soft pieces of linen, or else they hurt their fingers; and they are much longer over any stiff piece of calico. When thoroughly versed in hemming, they should learn to sew, which work should not be allowed in long and deep stitches, or too slanting, as is often the case in schools. In sewing, the teacher should be particular in making the child double back her work over the nail of her fore finger. When able to hem and sew well they should make a pinafore.

Before teaching a child how to back-stitch, they should learn how to run and fell, so as to make the seams quite neat on both sides, not to have any raw edges. When this is well understood, then put the child into back-stitching and button hole stitch, without knowing which it would be useless to attempt to make a shirt. The child should be shown how to draw her thread in stitching, for if

---

* Communicated by a lady.

she trusts to her eye she will invariably work crookedly, and have her stitches of uneven lengths. Above all they should never be allowed to take up a pencil and mark their work. It is a very bad and idle plan. The herring-bone stitch should then be taught.

As soon as the pupils are well versed in these different stitches, let them learn to cut out shifts, petticoats, shirts, and frocks; for a girl is only half taught who is obliged to get another person to measure and cut out her clothes.

There are nineteen parts in a shirt, and before it is begun to be put together I should make each girl understand thoroughly every one of those parts; how they are made and how joined together.

Darning is another important step, for what looks so ill as to see stockings, &c., looking as if those who mended them, had darned for the first time in their lives. A good way to learn to darn is, to begin on a piece of yellow canvas (yellow, because on that colour long, irregular stitches are more visible), neither fine nor coarse, but a medium texture.

SCHOOL HOURS, ETC.

The school hours would probably be these. From the 1st of May to the 1st of October the children should arrive at eight o'clock, *certainly not later* at that season. It is absurd to encourage late hours for working children, or indeed for any children. It is a mistake to open school at the usual hours. At 12·30 the non-working children are dismissed, and the workers clean themselves for dinner. Dinner at 12·40. From 1 to 2 play ground; it being optional for the working boys to resume their work during this hour instead of playing. The non-working children to have permission to assemble in the play ground at 1, or, under certain regulations, to bring their own dinner when they come in the morning, and dine with the working children. This should, by all means, be encouraged; but it should be expressly provided that they do not bring with them better fare than the working children have. Possibly arrangements might be made for cooking the provender so brought. It would, probably, be always a little more than the providers could eat, and the extra work (if any), would be compensated by the extra contribution to the general meal. After consulting several practical persons on this scheme, I am convinced it might be made to work well in all respects. The school beginning at 2 should close not later than 6 o'clock. An arrangement might then be made to give some of the working boys bread and cheese, on condition that they worked one or two hours longer when occasion required. Those turned twelve years would be able to do so perfectly well. In all out door labour these extra supplies of work must depend much on season and weather. It is impossible to lay down cast-iron rules as to the apportionment of the work to be done daily.

The selection of boys for the working staff must be determined by age, strength, and inclination. If the land will not support so large a number as are ready to work, a selection should be made according to merit. It should be held as the post of honour, as it will assuredly be that earnestly desired and sought for by the boys themselves, or they will be very different boys to any I have yet met with in the course of tolerably extensive experience. In the industrial workhouse schools in my district (extending over a fifth part of the kingdom for the last four years) I have found it universally felt as a severe punishment not to allow a boy to work when he has misbehaved himself: though occasionally parents will be found to object from vanity, but this will rarely happen. From the 1st of February to the 1st of April, and from the 1st of October till the 1st of December, the arrival hour may be 8·30; from the 1st of December till the 1st of February, at 9 o'clock, the other hours always remaining unchanged.

OTHER EMPLOYMENTS.

As it will be the object of these schools to train and
to educate children destined for country pursuits in such a
way as to make them good labourers and prosperous cot-
tagers, so that they shall not only acquire habits of industry
and means of livelihood, but such knowledge of useful arts
as may conduce hereafter to improve their stock of comforts and welfare of their household, it is expedient to give
them some knowledge of common handicrafts. The boys
at the Ealing school used to perform nearly all the work
that was required to be done on the premises. To a cot-
tager, there is no knowledge more useful than that of carpentering, shoemaking, and tailoring. In addition to bare
necessaries, our labourers and mechanics rarely have the
means of supplying the small comforts which add to the
decencies of life, and minister to independence. The
leisure hours spent at home will supply them when the
labourer has skill enough to cultivate his garden; its
vegetables add greatly to his table, while the flowers
nourish a sense of beauty, and contribute to the cheerfulness of his dwelling. A very small number of carpenters'
tools, if he has learnt to use them, would keep his furniture
in order and his house in neatness, enabling him to construct cupboards, shelves, screens, clothes-chests, &c.;
while the power of mending clothes and shoes would
materially lessen his expenditure, and add to the comfort
and respectable appearance of himself and his family. For
this purpose there should be a carpenter's, as well as a shoemaker's and tailor's shop, besides the bakehouse and
kitchen at the school. During the winter months and the
wet days, time might be thus most usefully occupied
which is now wasted in knitting or idling. It should be
an inflexible rule, that there should be no unemployed

time. It should be a course of almost incessant industry from morning till night. This is no hardship to the children, but quite the reverse. They all delight in industrial pursuits. The boys should, in rotation, pass a certain number of hours in each of the shops, and also work in turn at all the various occupations in the farm of which they were capable; each being duly explained to them, as well as performed by them; for it is all important that the industry be *instructional*, and that each child be shown *how* to do every thing in the best way, and also that he should learn *why* it is done so. Variety of work is essential to prevent fatigue, and due care must be taken to apportion it in kind, as well as amount, to the strength of the child.

Cheerfulness should be imparted to labour, and for this purpose vocal music is most useful. It not only relieves fatigue, and prevents weariness, but it cherishes good sentiments and kindly feelings.

Its great influence over bodies of men, especially in the effects of the vocal chorus of the German armies, has been often noted. The young are even more impressible by music than adults.

Singing is a natural gratification to most children; and they ought not to be debarred from it, for it is not only an innocent but an improving taste. The children in district schools should be taught to improve this faculty, and strike up a merry song as they go forth to and return from their work.

In the appropriation of shop-work to the children, some regard should be had to their natural capacity, just as in the school-room. The carpenter's shop should always exist; and the schoolmaster and pupil teacher must take lessons of the village carpenter for a couple of hours daily, if they really have had such a curious bringing up as not to know how to manage a few ordinary tools. There will be no expense in the carpenter's shop; the making and mending of fences, tools, and the doing of all kinds of odd jobs, will fully repay the small amount of wood to be purchased, and the Committee of Council makes grants for the tools. To erect a hut for the shop, or to convert some outbuilding into it, would be part of the work to be done. The shoemaker's department might possibly give some trouble and expense, and would require a shoemaker to teach the boys. This might be managed by means of a small extra payment for those who learned it.

The growth and preparation of flax is strongly recommended by Mr. Warne of Suffolk, who has written much and ably on the subject. Rope-making and mat-making are both occupations which are suitable to wet weather.

The ground labour is so important that it must be the subject of a separate chapter.

It is also very desirable that there should be a hand corn-mill purchased, to grind the flour for the bread. Cobbett, in his inimitable work on *Cottage Economy*, says about this :—

What I would recommend to gentlemen with considerable families, or to farmers, is a mill, such as I myself have at present. With this mill, turned by a man and a stout boy, I can grind six bushels of wheat in a day, and dress the flour. The grinding of six bushels of wheat, at ninepence a bushel, comes to four and sixpence, which pays the man and the boy, supposing them (which is not, and seldom can be, the case) to be hired for the express purpose out of the street. With this same mill you grind meat for your pigs, and of this, you will get eight or ten bushels ground in a day. You have no trouble about sending to the mill; you are sure to have your *own wheat*, for, strange as it may seem, I used sometimes to find that I sent white Essex wheat to the mill, and that it brought me flour from very coarse red wheat. There is no accounting for this, except by supposing that wind and water power has something in it to change the very nature of the grain; as when I came to grind by horses, such as the wheat went into the hopper, so the flour came out into the bin.   *   *   *   The cost of this mill is twenty pounds. The dresser is four more; the horse-path and wheel might possibly be four or five more; and I am very certain that to any farmer living at a mile from a mill, having twelve persons in family, having forty pigs to feed, and twenty hogs to fatten, the savings of such a mill would pay the whole expenses of it the very first year.

A bakehouse is the next requisite. The girls and a strong boy will assist the schoolmistress in making and working the bread. It should, of course, be all made and baked at home.

It may be anticipated, that many a benevolent clergyman and other promoter, will, when he shall have got so far, say to himself, why should not the girls have similar training? A washing and ironing house arise in the vista by the side of the bakehouse, and the children allowed to wash their own things, finding of course every expense. Thus, what admirable housewives and provident little wives will be furnished for the coming generation; able not only to make and mend their own and children's clothes (now a rare accomplishment), but to be dairy maids, to cook nicely, and to make bread, and eke to bake it too. Will not there be lots of good and handy *servants* besides, whom every body will be glad to have from this useful sort of school?

Whether in-door or out-door, the ruling principle of the establishment should be *to make the children themselves do all work.* Their pursuits would be chiefly the following:—

Boys.	Girls.
1. Spade husbandry in all its branches.	1. Household work of all kinds,* including cooking.
2. Attending to the cattle, pigs, &c.	2. Dairy work (for eldest girls).
3. Shoemaking, baking.	3. Washing and ironing (idem).
4. Preparation of flax for the spinners.	4. Needlework.
	5. Spinning flax.

* The school teachers should always live on the premises, and the working girls will thus have ample means of learning all kinds of household work.

Moral training should pervade the entire system of labour and instruction from morning till night. The practice of true religion should imbue the whole system. The teachers, moreover, I repeat, must be fitted to obtain a hold on the *hearts* of the children. There can be no efficient moral discipline without it.

That which the play-ground is to Mr. Stowe's system of discipline in town schools, the farm and the handicrafts will be to these schools. It is there that the ideal will become the real, and that application will be given to the lessons of the school and the fireside. It is the nursery-ground where the young trees are placed for nurture and development previously to their transplantation into the world. For want of this practical adaptation of instruction to conduct, this training of the faculties, as well as storing of the head, nine-tenths of our existing schools are nearly useless, and, in many cases, do more harm than good.

The great deficiency in the instruction of our poorer classes, is in that sort of practical knowledge of the ordinary objects and operations, both of nature and art, which it is most useful to them to understand; a want of acquaintance, not with those branches of knowledge which do *not*, but which *do* belong to their condition in life and to their daily avocations.

We must now devote a chapter to the management of the land; but cannot better close this than by citing the following testimony to the practicability of the scheme, from the last report of the Rev. Mr. Bellairs, who cites instances of its adoption in some part of his large district in the western counties:—

Adverting to some former remarks, a well-arranged system of manual employment, in connexion with our present schools, especially if in any respect reproductive, would have the effect not only of retaining children at school to a higher age than is now the case, but if the employments were those of the locality in which the school is situate, would fit them for their future occupations. In manufacturing and town districts there would be, as I before observed, greater difficulty in making the necessary arrangements for giving instruction in the various employments of a locality. But in such places this varied instruction would be the less necessary, inasmuch as so far as the children are concerned, superior intelligence would compensate for the absence of particular manual dexterity. And I think it probable that some common works of industry might be cultivated, which should sufficiently exercise the muscles for general purposes, leaving them to secure hereafter dexterity in any particular branch to which they might be called.

This would not be the case in agricultural districts, for there the children would require to be acclimatized by outdoor work, in order to endure inclemency of weather. But in such districts industrial occupations are comparatively easy of arrangement; a small piece of ground, a few spades, rakes, and hoes, a master moderately acquainted with horticulture, and some scientific work upon gardening, form all the requisites for, at all events, the commencement of such outdoor occupations.

In addition to this, if a carpenter's or a blacksmith's shop was added, of course additional opportunities of securing information and practice would be afforded. This last appendage has been introduced during the last year at Hagley, by the Hon. and Rev. W. Lyttelton, and from the general character of the school I do not doubt of its success.

Connected with this subject, at this school, Hagley, a plan has been adopted which I think is likely to exercise a very favourable influence on the girls there. Certain ladies in the parish take under their patronage certain girls in the school, who attend on stated days at their houses, for the purpose of learning practically some of the most important parts of domestic work; in this way they are instructed in washing, making bread, cleaning furniture, &c., and thus in many respects prepared for domestic service.

Such a plan, independent of its advantages in improving the industrial habits of these girls, will have a considerable influence on their character, and tend to bind the employer and employed more closely together—a point by no means to be undervalued.

The three schools in this district in which manual industrial occupations are most successfully carried out, are Hagley, Cubington, and Forthampton. To Cubington your Lordships have been pleased to make a grant of 9l. 15s., on this account; 2l. 5s. as a gratuity to the master for superintending the agricultural department; and 7l. 10s. to the managers for purchase of tools.

Lord Lyttelton has written to me thus of his schools very lately, in reply to my inquiry whether any disadvantages had resulted from this system:—

I am not aware of the slightest disadvantages attending them. They seem to have produced some effect in keeping boys for some time longer at school than they might otherwise have remained, and I should suppose they are beneficial in a more direct manner in instilling into them some knowledge of gardening, &c.; but perhaps we can hardly judge of that yet. They find their own seeds and plants, but pay no rent: I give them tools and manure, from which they get no small profit.

CHAPTER II.

The School Farm.

" THE farm" sounds rather grandly, especially as I mean to confine my estimates and remarks to four and a-half acres, which puts our operations on rather a homœopathic scale, and relieve farmers of any painful amount of alarm at the effect we shall be likely to produce on the agricultural interest. This is as well, as we hope to have a good deal of kind aid, and many useful hints, from the experience of those around our little establishments. We shall not fail to be rather proud of their notice, and of any little encouragement they may be pleased to give to our humble labours.

It must always be remembered that we do not aim at giving the children a finished education in farming, but simply an aptitude and handiness for labour. We want to establish schools of useful industry, not agricultural colleges.

The object of the cultivation of the land besides that of training the children, is to pay for their dinners, and leave perhaps a small surplus as a perquisite for the master; or if this be arranged otherwise, towards a school fund. Let us see how this can be done.

It is so obvious that any system of cultivation, and its results, must depend so mainly on the soil and on the skill bestowed on it, that it is almost hazardous to put forth any general scheme or calculation. It would not, however, suffice to leave the matter to mere assertion. That the land may be well made to supply what we require from it, any market gardener would be able to vouch for, and would give information how to crop it in his way, as the farmer would how to farm it with a degree of skill which would render it quite needless to say any thing about it here, were we going to adopt either of their systems. That, however, which has been found to answer best for schools, is a system distinct from either.

After much consideration of the matter, and taking counsel from experienced men on the subject, it seems that *the cultivation of light loam land by spade husbandry, with liquid manure*, will be at once the most profitable for the school and beneficial to the children. The liquid manure which results from a large establishment, and which is in many cases now thrown away, is a certain source of largely increased produce from land. Then again, the labour of boys being used for certain minute operations in the cultivation of the crops, as well as in digging and preparing the soil, is, as has been said, another source of increased produce. This will give, if properly managed, on a sufficient quantity of land, a return which may be made to cover all expenses from the dinners of such a school, *over and above* the cost *now* incurred, and which of course must continue to be paid whether there be a dinner or not.

Supposing the four acres to be arable, and the half acre meadow, it will be advisable to keep at least two or three cows stall-fed, and as many pigs as there is food for. This is the quantity of land, and the system adopted at the Quatt school for several years, and the accounts there have been kept with great accuracy.*

The cropping and rotation of crops must necessarily vary with the character of the soil ; but, in the ordinary run of loam soil, the following has been found to be applicable and productive. I shall here avail myself of the report I have already made to the Lords of the Committee of Council on this subject, laid before Parliament in 1849, with such additions and corrections as subsequent experience or information have supplied, and adapted to the object immediately in view.

I may briefly state, that every research I make for reliable information on this point confirms my original view, that no system will afford so much useful instructional employment and moral training for the boys, and even for the girls, or so much profitable produce for the establishment, as one which shall comprise the following elements :—

1st. A dairy farm.
2nd. A loam soil.
3rd. Cultivated by spade husbandry exclusively.
4th. Crops :—Roots and green crops, Italian rye grasses, &c.,
        garden vegetables, and *no grain crops*.
5th. A small proportion of meadow land.
6th. Good milking cows, increasing with the crops, to be
        exclusively stall-fed.
7th. As many pigs as there is food for.
8th. Drains in the cow-stalls so arranged as to collect every
        atom of manure from the cows, and likewise from the
        pig-cots, the stable, and the house ; to run into tanks,

---

* I make the assertion with perfect confidence, notwithstanding the unjust attacks made on it by a very few persons, who chose to assume that it was pretended that this establishment was self-supporting, just as if 60 or 70 mouths ; and by others, who wilfully misrepresented the accounts published. They have been thoroughly tested, and are quite trustworthy.

to be skilfully prepared and applied by water-cart to the land and growing crops, and especially to the grasses.

9th. Mineral manures skilfully applied.

10th. Gorse to be grown in all the hedge-rows and waste corners for the cows.*

11th. Flax, to a moderate extent, for food for the cows, and for manufacture in the winter by the children of both sexes.†

12th. Vegetables for the house consumption, to be also liquid manured, potatoes excepted.

13th. The growth of seeds for sale and use.

The arable land may be divided into seven equal parts, if flax is to be grown, and into six if it is not. In the former case, there will be ninety-one poles to each crop, in the latter nearly one hundred and seven.

The rotation would be as follows :—*First year, wurzels and swedes.* Ridge land in November, and in spring redig, and manure both solid and liquid. This crop well repays it. Sow wurzels in April, by dibbling rows in small ridges, well apart, and each plant eighteen inches. Take especial care that the wurzel seed when trodden in is not more than an inch deep in the ground, or it will never come up. Two or three seeds in each hole. Steep seed for twenty-four hours before sowing. More liquid manure when plants are young. Thin the leaves in July. Take up in October or November.

NB. If the flies attack these plants, or swedes, nothing is so good as *wood* ashes. It will effectually destroy them. Coal ashes will do.

Second year, potatoes. The land would be ridged as before, in the previous December. In March, it would be manured, dug, and planted. The crop would be off by the latter end of August. In September the ground would

---

* See Paper by Richard Spooner, Esq., M.P., on its uses. Appendix E.

† See a little work by J. Warne, Esq., of Norfolk, and also by George Nicholls, Esq., on its culture.

be well dug, and manured, and Italian rye-grass sown as soon as possible.

Third year, Italian rye-grass. The first cutting would be about the first week in May; the second in twenty-five days afterwards; and a third, fourth, and fifth* would follow at intervals of nearly a month each, till the early frosts set in. After each cutting the plants must be well watered with liquid manure. In December the land would be dug, and ridged as before, but *not* manured.

Fourth year, flax. The land should be dug over early in April, but not manured. The seed should be in as soon as the frost disappears. The crop would be off early in July, and a catch crop of rape, after digging in solid manure, might be obtained the same winter, which would be ready in the following February or March.

Fifth year, carrots, or parsnips and turnips. The ground should be dug, but not manured, as soon as the last crop was off. Sow immediately then, in August, and the crop would be off the ground during the month of November. Ridge and manure in December.

Sixth year, cabbages. Dig and manure, and plant in March. Crop off the ground by end of August. Manure and dig in September, or sow vetches and clover.

Seventh year, vetches or clover. Crop in May and June. Another catch crop might then be taken before sowing the wurzels.*

There will, of course, under any circumstances, be some modification of this scheme. By reducing the number of perches to each crop, a portion of land might be reserved for onions, parsley, spinach, and a variety of small vegetables, which it is useful to cultivate. Also for flowers.

Drains and Tank. The estimates of produce which are

---

* Mr. Dickenson, of Curzon-street, May-fair, had ten cuttings in one year.

to follow, depend mainly on this mine of agricultural wealth, and their due arrangement is thus important. There should be one or two tanks, according to the number of the animals, &c. One for the excreta of all the animals, and another, quite distinct, for the privies and house drains. There are different properties in these; and Mr. Johnston's excellent works on the subject are beginning to give us an insight into their due uses.

The reservoirs should contain at least 500 gallons. They may be about twelve feet deep, and five or six in diameter. This is the best proportion. Common labourers can construct them. The floor is either composed of brick or of stone work, embedded in grey lime mortar, and coated with Parker's cement—no clay being used in any part of the tank. The sides are circular, and are walled up in the same manner ; and the top or dome is then built by circular layers of bricks, flint, or chalk, resting on the top of the side wall, each course advancing one-third of their length beyond the previous layers, which are regularly backed in, during the progress of the work, by the earth. The top, or aperture, is secured by slabs of wood or mason work a foot or two high. A pump of iron, or wood,* for drawing out the liquid, is inserted ; so as to be easily removable and cleaned, if choked up.

A still cheaper tank may be made, by sinking two or three old oil casks, which, if iron hooped, will last a few years. They should communicate *at the bottom* by short lead pipes.

The drains should be so constructed as to bring into these tanks all the refuse, wash, and liquid of every description from the house, together with the night-soil of the out-buildings and the excreta of the pigs' cots, of which

---

* These may be made for 15s., of deal, about six inches square. If bound with iron hoop, they will last a long time.

latter the floors should be made to slant for the purpose of facilitating their drainage.* By far the most valuable part of the liquid manure results from the cowstalls; and this is one reason why dairy farms on this system are the most lucrative, owing to the return they yield to the land for the produce they derive from it.

I am inclined to think that the mode of constructing drains in the cowstalls of Switzerland and Germany presents advantages for school farms. The cattle stand on inclined floors flagged with tiles, bricks, or planks, to which latter there is an objection. At the lowest part of this inclined plane (it should be slightly inclined only at the heels, or rather beyond them), close to the heels of the cows, runs a gutter along the whole length of the stalls. It should be about nine inches deep by nine inches in width; this trench should communicate with the reservoir at one end. The trench should have a sluice door at the end next to the tank, in order that its contents may be retained for a few days before they are voided into the tank. Such portion of the *excreta* of the cattle as does not fall or drain itself into the trench, may be raked and swept into it, or used as solid dung.

The next process is to pour a quantity of water into the trench. The object of this is not only to liquify the manure, and increase the quantity, but to assist the chemical process it must undergo. By this means the water in the trench, in the first place, keeps the air cool, and free from the effluvia which would otherwise arise. Cow-stalls on this principle are much freer from odour than on the ordinary system, without trenches. This is, however, the least of its advantages. In the ordinary process of putrefaction which the manure, and especially the urine, undergoes, the escape of ammonia, in the form of gas, occasions

---

* I have found by experience that this may be overdone.

a considerable loss of the richest element of its manuring property. It is, therefore, very important to add to the compost some substance of an acid quality which may combine with the ammonia as it is generated, and neutralize and retain it.

The manuring properties of the liquid may be further increased by the addition of green copperas, humus (sulphate of iron), or the alum of commerce, which generates sulphate of ammonia, which is one of the strongest saline manures in existence. When the trench is full, it is well stirred; the sluice door is opened, and it empties itself into the tank, where it remains till the putrefactive fermentation is complete, and the caustic qualities of the ammonia (destructive to vegetable life) are removed.

When all the ammonia is thoroughly saturated with, and fixed by the carbonic acid, it has arrived at its proper maturity. The period varies with the atmosphere. Three months always suffices; 44 cows will yield on this process full 30,000 hogsheads of liquid, besides the straw dung, every year. The mixture thus prepared may be applied in autumn, winter, and spring, not only on the rye-grass, but on barley and rape, when they are a foot high, without injury. It may be applied to almost any growing crop with benefit. This cannot be done with solid manure, which can alone be applied to the land itself prior to the sowing of the crops, and a period of one or two years elapses before complete decomposition ensues. The growing plant, on the contrary, absorbs the salts and nutritive properties of the liquid manure, imparted to it by direct contact and without diminution or delay.

Much depends on the equal distribution of the liquid over a field. I venture, therefore, to append the following suggestions as to the means of doing this:—

The liquid is pumped from the tank into the water-cart, of which the following is the best and simplest description, being at once lighter and stronger than those usually adopted. A common wine-pipe will supply the cask, and the carriage may be constructed by the commonest work-man. The cart can be drawn by a strong pony, or it may be made lighter still, so as to be drawn by hand. The following sectional elevation and plan are drawn to a scale of a quarter of an inch to a foot. The wheels should have broad fellies, in order not to cut deep when drawn over the land and crops. The flow of the liquid is best effected by plac-ing a flat board opposite the spout in a slanting direction, with ribs of wood nailed on to it in a fan shape, in order to spread the liquid; the liquid falling thereon, splashes and distributes itself in the best manner on the land or crops. The ribs are about an inch in height, and there is a narrow piece of wood nailed at right angles on the top, to prevent the liquid from splashing over.

A common plug is placed at the ordinary tap hole, and being withdrawn, the liquid rushes against the board; the advantage over the other plans being, that it not only

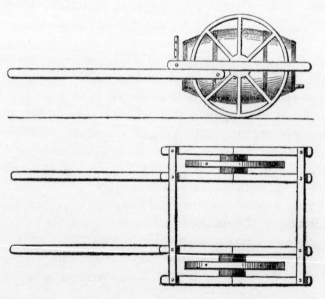

spreads the liquid perfectly, but it throws it under the cart, and is therefore more cleanly to use.

As there are no holes for the liquid to run through, as in water carts, however thick, it cannot choke.*

Mr. Sillett, in his 'Practical Hints,' suggests and uses the following barrow, which appears to be well adapted for small plots of ground, as it can be managed by one man or boy with ease.

The little apparatus at the left hand handle A, enables the driver to lower the barrel forwards. B is a trough which receives the liquid, and the opening or slit at the bottom can be enlarged or lessened by means of the screw C, so as to regulate the flow of the liquid. This is made by Messrs. Ransome and May of Ipswich.

The other tools required are the light spades and forks and the Derbyshire hoe, which Mr. Sillett strongly recommends, and with good reason. Here it is.

This is an excellent tool for cleansing and loosening the ground between growing crops.

---

* It can also be put on with garden-engines or watering-pots.

Here also is a most useful tool for lightening sub-soil without the trouble of double digging.

SUB-SOIL PRONG.

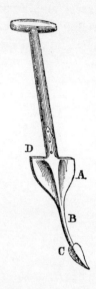

The handle and shaft are like those of a spade, but made straight; the length of the handle being 32 inches, and that of the lower part 20 inches, consisting of a bar of iron made about $\frac{5}{8}$ of an inch, in thickness by $1\frac{1}{2}$ inch, so as to present as little resistance to the soil as possible, but terminating with a flat spear-like head, C, which operates on the sub-soil only. A is a flat piece of iron about 5 inches wide, in order to bear on the top soil, which acts as a fulcrum. It is thrust down into the ground like a spade, and the foot being placed on the bar D, the handle is depressed, just as in digging, only that no attempt is made to lift the soil, the handle being depressed about 2 feet the work is done, for the spear head, operated on by the lever power, has disturbed the sub-soil and opened it. It should be used at $1\frac{1}{2}$ feet distances both ways to act effectually, or in lighter soils 2 feet. It can of course be used when the plants are growing, and between them as well as before they are put in. I can attest its practical usefulness. This invention is due to Mr. Crutchley, the master of the Market Drayton workhouse, whose ingenious inventions and skill in gardening have raised produce far exceeding what I have calculated on for farm schools, but no more than the same appliances may produce anywhere with fair soil to work on. The spear point 'comes' about 3 inches.

So much for tools.

The course of cropping has been adopted with reference not only to the food required for the animals, but for the dinners which the potatoes, parsnips, carrots, turnips, and part of the cabbage, besides the smaller vegetables, will directly supply.

The Italian rye-grass is one of the most prolific crops known. It has been cut by Mr. Dickenson, of May Fair, London, ten times in the year; four times is under the average. It is, in fact, a condensed meadow, supplying the use of four times the same amount of grass through the summer months. Adopt it whenever the meadow land is insufficient. The meadow should be made into hay, if possible; two crops got off it by liquid manuring.*

Cows always require a little hay to amuse them when milking, and also to digest the roots which will form their staple food through the whole of the winter months. By no means omit the swedes. They should be given with the wurzel, in the proportion of two swedes and three wurzels (and so grown). These swedes counteract the watery and aperient properties of the wurzel, which alone impoverishes the milk; and the wurzels counteract the too stimulating properties of the swede, and prevent them from affecting the taste of the milk, which, however, may be also prevented by that extreme and spotless cleanliness which is all important in the dairy, churn, and pans.

The pigs will supply plenty of fresh pork and bacon.

The butter or the milk should be all sold. It fetches a fair price anywhere, if good. In towns, a great deal more may be made usually by milk than butter, but some should always be made, if only to teach the little maidens how.†

---

* It is most important that it should be well drained, if needed. See an economical mode of doing this in Mr. Sillett's pamphlet.

† If the dairy is carried to any extent, a dairy-maid will be required, whose keep and wages it will then repay.

As the dairy is the great source of the produce, it is important to ascertain what amount of food is requisite for stall-fed cows. An experiment has been made, and it is from its result that my estimate has been made of the number of cows which could be maintained by stall-feeding from the roots and seeds derivable from the land in question. It has been found that a stall-fed cow, well supplied with food, consumes in twenty-four hours no less than from 150 to 170 lbs. weight of green-meat in summer, and 150 lbs. of roots in winter, with a very small quantity of hay, some of which I think would be obtained from the clovers and rye-grass. The breeds most esteemed for milking appear to be the Yorkshire and Irish; and middled-sized cows are generally deemed the most advantageous, as yielding more milk in proportion to their feed than the large heavy cows.

There are few branches of husbandry which are more lucrative than that of dairy farms. It is not easy to ascertain from tenant farmers the amount of produce attainable from a cow. Their yield in quantity of milk, and again, in its quality, varies very greatly. I have heard of well-attested instances where 28*l.* and 30*l.* have been made in a single year by the calf and milk of a single cow, in other cases it will not exceed 10*l.*; but *if due care be taken and a fair price paid for good milkers*, there is no doubt that an average of 16*l.* is below rather than above the gross annual value of the produce of a fair cow. Always buy young cows with a calf by their side, sell the calf, and sell the cow when dry, and buy again, unless you get a first-rate milker. Buy Mr. Cuthbert Johnson's little book on the *Modern Dairy*,* and attend to all he says. The mode of feeding, milking, and managing cows at Quatt,

---

* Published by Ridgway, price 3*s.* 6*d.*

where great success has resulted, was thus described lately by one of the boys employed there:—

The length of the cowhouse is 24 feet 6 inches, in which there stand three cows, one pony, and a part for the calves' cot. The standing-place for each cow is 4 feet 2 inches, which leaves 8 feet 4 inches for the pony, and 3 feet 8 inches for the calves' cot.

The width is 16 feet 6 inches, out of which there is 3 feet 1 inch for passage before cows, to give them their food, 2 feet 4 inches for feeding troughs, 7 feet 6 inches for standing-place for each cow, and 3 feet 7 inches for causeway behind them.

The drains run into a large tank which lies west of the cowhouse, and holds 1400 gallons, and also receives the drainage from the privies, pigsties, and washhouse, which lie south of the cowhouse.

The cows are always tied up, summer and winter, except for an hour or two, when they are let into a piece of ground about a quarter of an acre in size, for the purpose of airing and exercise.

Their food is carried to them, and consists of wurzels, carrots, hay, swedes, cabbage, vetches, rape, and Italian rye-grass, the latter of which is cut three or four times during the year. The first green crop that comes into use is rape, which is sown the previous autumn, and comes into use about March; after that vetches, which were sown last October; after that, early cabbage and grass, carried to them with a little hay. We then find ourselves at about midsummer, at which time we have plenty of green food, such as grass, oxcabbages, thinnings of the wurzels and carrots, &c. We then give them wurzel leaves stripped off and carried to them, with a little grass and hay, which lasts till about November. We then give them wurzels and carrot-tops, with the remainder of the cabbages, with a little grass, and about 8 lbs. of hay per day, which last till about this time, when we have to depend upon the roots through the winter till March, when the green food comes in again. The following is an account of the cows dietary:—

At 5 o'clock in the morning, they have 28 lbs. wurzels, which last till milking time. After milking they have a few swedes.

At 9 o'clock they have a little hay, and then go to water.

At 12 o'clock they have 28 lbs. carrots.

At 4 o'clock they have 28 lbs. wurzels.

At 6 o'clock they are milked, and then have a few swedes.

At 8 o'clock they have 28 lbs. carrots.

At 9 o'clock they are supped up with hay, and left for the night.

The cultivation of flax appears to afford a prospect of success on school farms, both as regards the value of its seed for feeding cattle, the saleability of, and profit derivable from the flax itself, as well as the employment in the operations of steeping, stacking, scutching, and spinning it affords to the children. The annual value of the crop varies considerably; the flax averages from 20*l.* to 25*l.* per acre, and the seed from 5*l.* to 6*l.*, in Flanders; but in England it will usually fetch much more. It appears from the following work on flax in *Flemish Husbandry*, published by the 'Society for the Diffusion of Useful Knowledge,' that by the system of husbandry I propose to adopt, very large crops may be fairly reckoned on:—

For this purpose a surplus of tillage and manure is given to each crop, so that the soil is deepened and ameliorated at each successive step, and is brought to as perfect a state as it will admit of by the time the turn comes to sow flax. This may remove the surprise which is naturally excited by the amount of tillage and manure given for each crop, which appears at first sight far greater than can be required. The quantity of liquid manure poured over the light lands, year after year, cannot fail to make them rich, and the frequent trenching with the spade must, in the end, transform the whole soil, to a considerable depth, into a compost of rich vegetable and animal matter, intimately mixed with the natural earths. It is, in fact, an accumulation of humus, which is the best preparation to ensure a good crop of flax. It is not, therefore, to the immediate preparation of the soil for the flax that its abundance or good quality is to be chiefly ascribed, but to a gradual system of amelioration, which has brought the soil into the high condition required for this plant.

The following books are strongly recommended, as containing admirable rules, and most valuable information on all points required for the successful cultivation of the ground, and the management of the stock and crops, as well on the subject of spade husbandry, as on the management of cows, pigs, &c. :—

The Classbook on Agriculture, by The Irish Society.

C. Johnston's Book on the Management of the Dairy Cow.

Sillett's Practical System of Fork and Spade Husbandry. A Shilling Pamphlet, with Drawings of Tools.

Manual of Field Gardening. (Simpkin and Marshall.)

The Finchley Manual of Industry.—On Gardening.

Cottage Gardening. (A reprint from *The Agricultural Journal.*) By James Main, A.L.S. Printed by W. Clowes & Son, London.

The Flax Grower. By George Nicholls, Esq. Knight, London.

Stephens on Field Gardening.

EXPENSES.

The expence of the children's dinner will average, from actual experiment, about tenpence per week per head. If it much exceeds this, either an extravagant price is given for the food, or too large a proportion of meat, which need not exceed five ounces each, twice a week.*

On the amount of land we have taken as our estimate, four acres and a half, there would be probably thirteen working boys, and say four working girls, to feed. The produce of the land, after deducting all expenses, could, according to the actual experiments made (of which some fair specimens of the results are given in Appendix D), scarcely fail to pay for the dinners of these children. Supposing, however, that it did; it would, at any rate, more than suffice for the allowance to the parents of some return for the labour of their children.

Thus would the great object be attained, of giving the parents such an interest in the child's labour as would reconcile them to it, and also to his longer stay at school.

When the land is brought, on this system, into full bearing, the produce is often far beyond the amount calculated on here.

---

* They would be pretty sure to have it also on Sundays at home.

Farmers, indeed, who are accustomed to the results only of plough husbandry, are very incredulous of high returns. Their judgment is based on a system of cultivation which costs comparatively very little labour, and makes proportionably small produce. This is a system which requires, and has the advantage of a great deal of labour, and proportionably large produce. ' Ay,' says the farmer, ' but look at the cost of this extra labour.' We do look, and beg him to look : the boys supply it—boys who were idle before. It costs *nothing*. And so far from its being incredible that hearty and healthy boys and girls, with skill to direct them, can earn their own dinners, it would be incredible that they could *not*, and a great deal more besides.

There is a capital required to start with; but, as regards stock, it should not be too large at first. Tools, moreover, are not expensive. But for these things grants are obtainable, and also in aid of the schoolmaster's salary in virtue of his industrial superintendence.

It is scarcely necessary to go into the various modes whereby a smaller adoption of the industrial system might be accomplished by a smaller amount of land and fewer animals; or by nothing beyond a vegetable garden, from which there might or might not be funds enough to give the dinner. The best mode of raising a large enough return to do so in this case, would be by growing and selling agricultural seeds. They are, when really genuine, always saleable, and fetch good prices. At the Quatt school an experiment was made last year, which yielded a very astonishing produce, far exceeding 30*l*. per acre. This hint will prove worth attention. The watching, collecting, sorting, and subsequent care required of the seeds, will afford plenty of useful occupation to the children.

Where a dinner is impracticable, it will be always necessary to give the children a return for the labour, either in kind, by a share of the produce, or in money, to the parents.

By some one, therefore, of the several scales and schemes suggested, it is humbly hoped that the practicability of industrial farm schools, at least for any country locality, has been demonstrated ; and if the temporal means are thus easy, and the return ample, the true friends of education may rely on it, that the moral fruits will be tenfold more so.

APPENDIX.

A.

MISSTATEMENTS OF INCREASE OF SCHOOLS.

As an example of the reckless manner in which it has been attempted to mislead the public as to the increase of schools, by some of the opponents of State aid, Mr. Edward Baines commences his fourth letter, addressed a few years ago to Lord John Russell, with this passage :

' I believe I shall be able to show, to the conviction of every candid man, that the prevalent notions concerning the insufficiency of the means of education in this country are extremely erroneous,—that the impression which Dr. Hook's pamphlet is calculated to produce on this subject is exceedingly wide of the truth,—and that no deficiency exists which the people themselves, without any parliamentary compulsion, are not able with ease to supply.'

He arrives at the conclusion that day schools were required, when he wrote in 1846, for 1,945,111 children, from which he does not deduct the children of the middle and higher classes.

Mr. Baines avails himself of the Returns of Education in 1833, which resulted as follows :—

' EDUCATION IN ENGLAND AND WALES.

Scholars in Infant Schools	89,005
,, in Daily Schools.	1,187,942
Total in Infant and Daily Schools	1,276,947
Scholars in Sunday Schools . . .	1,548,890 '

Mr. Baines adopts this return without any remark as to what classes of day schools it comprises. And as he afterwards adds to it those established by grants from the Privy Council Office, which are exclusively given to schools for the humbler classes, the inference at first is that Earl Kerry's returns relate also to such schools only. Now in the very page before that in which the summary is given in the report (p. 1331), under the head of 'Remarks on the Summary in England and Wales,' the following clause is conspicuously printed:—

'2. *Daily Schools*,—include Colleges (except those at Oxford and Cambridge), Grammar Schools, Boarding Schools, Proprietary, National and Lancasterian Schools, and Preparatory Schools of every description where the children remain beyond seven years of age.'

This passage occurs in the remarks which introduce the summary Mr. Baines adopts, and render it useless to his purpose. The return comprises, for instance, the great schools of 'Westminster,' 'Harrow,' 'Rugby,' 'Winchester,' &c. together, as he was informed, with every Boarding and Proprietary School in England, and yet, knowing this, he did not scruple to couple it, without note or comment, to an estimate of schools exclusively provided for the working classes, and he presents the whole as a statement of the amount of school accommodation for the humbler classes, accompanied by a positive assertion that it settles the question which relates exclusively to a deficiency of schools for the humbler classes—for of none other is there a question, and of none other was he treating. Not satisfied with this, he actually takes credit for a larger number of scholars than these Returns give,—talks about their 'incompleteness'—and on the score of some alleged omissions in three or four towns, sums up by saying,

'Thus, thirteen years back, we have official evidence of 1,276,947 children being in the Day Schools of England and Wales; but those numbers were confessedly *below the truth*,—in some important towns, to the extent of one-third.'

(To which he annexes as a note, what follows:)

'Probably two-thirds of the children in Infant Schools would be below five years of age; but, considering the *admitted defectiveness* of the returns, I shall be more than justified in considering the whole 1,276,947 children as of the school age.'

He proceeds to estimate the number of scholars for whom school *accommodation* has been afforded since 1833, and which is alleged to amount to 600,000 or 650,000, and says:—

'Let us take the *smaller* number, and add it to Lord Kerry's *incomplete* returns.

Day Scholars in England and Wales in 1833 . . 1,276,947
Schools provided since 1833 for 600,000

Total 1,876,947

'Here then, my Lord, are the results :—

Day Schools *Required* for 1,945,111
    ,,   *Existing* for 1,876,947

Present deficiency   68,164

' I lay those figures before your Lordship and the country.
What need I say more ?'

Mr. Baines' reason is now obvious for making no deduction
from the number who *ought* to be at school on account of those
who belong to the non-working classes. He intended to include
them in the returns of those who were *at* school in 1833. He
well knew that, inasmuch as there is no deficiency of schooling
for the richer class of children, those among them at school
would be a far larger proportion of the whole number there,
than they would of the total number of children of the school
age. He therefore omitted to deduct them from the number
who *ought* to be at school, in order to include them among those
who *are at* school, and the result is, whether intentional or not,
a gross mis-statement of the facts in question.

It is by aid of Dr. Hook's estimate (whose accuracy Mr. Baines,
in the former part of his letter, had demolished, but who now errs on
Mr. Baines' side of the question), and with the Minutes of Council
before him, that Mr. Baines arrives at the conclusion that the
number of scholars from 1833 till 1846 had increased by 600,000.

He says, ' Those schools would probably supply accommodation for 493,650 children, according to the average ratio of the
number of children to the grants of money observed in the
Minutes.'

The number which the schools, aided by these grants, are to
accommodate, is in each case published in the annual Minutes of
Council, and instead of being 'probably' for 493,650 children
and for 3,291 schools from 1833 to 1846, the numbers entered
opposite to each grant under the head of ' number of children to
be provided for in schools at six square feet each,' amount, from
1840 till 1846, to 271,461 children in 1280 schools.* This was,
it seems, the result of the grants of 1840—45, amounting during
that period, according to Dr. Hook, to 275,000*l.* In like proportion, the grants, from 1833—39, of 120,000*l.*, would provide
accommodation for 118,455 scholars and 558 schools, giving a

---

* This is of course exclusive of Scotch schools, but including all grants
for the enlargement as well as erection of schools in England and Wales.

total accommodation, from 1833 to 1846, for 389,916 scholars (instead of 493,650), and 1835 schools (instead of 3291). Dr. Hook sums up with the following wild supposition :—

' If we suppose (and this would be a liberal estimate) that 100 such private schools have been annually erected without Parliamentary aid since 1833, then 1300 elementary schools (the results of unaided private benevolence) must be added to 3291 schools built with public aid ; and *the proportionate number of scholars* ACCOMMODATED SINCE 1833 *may perhaps be raised to* 600,000 *or* 650,000. But this latter estimate must be regarded merely as an approximation to the truth.'—pp. 8, 9.

And this is termed 'a moderate and cautious calculation,' and forthwith adopted on the authority of a writer whose trustworthiness has just been demolished! Where are these 1300 schools erected by private benevolence in thirteen years without any aid from the state ? Can a quarter or even a tithe of them be named ? Can Dr. Hook ? I greatly doubt it. Until Mr. Baines or his authority does so, I must be pardoned for questioning the accuracy of the statement, which I believe to be sheer surmise.

Supposing even that Dr. Hook were right in his estimate of the number of scholars for which accommodation is provided since 1833, what has this to do with the question ? Mr. Baines undertook to show, not the area of schoolrooms, but " the number of scholars actually in the day schools.' I quote his own words (pp. 25 and 28.) Does it follow that because there are rooms built for a given number of scholars that that number are in them ? The reverse is, if not a necessary consequence, at least the probable result, for schoolrooms are usually built with view to an increase of numbers, and the complaints of schoolmasters are almost universal that the attendance is scanty and irregular. He is perpetually confusing the number of scholars with school accommodation, as if they meant the same thing. The question is as to the size and soundness of the kernel, and he makes a parade of shells and husks !

I shall not follow the example of making guesses at the number of children actually in the schools in question, being perfectly persuaded that no adequate means or record exist for ascertaining them,* but will recapitulate the blunders of this palpably exaggerated estimate. In the first place, Mr. Baines cites returns of the scholars in schools of *every* description as

* The returns in the late census are not yet published, but when they are, we shall, perhaps, have but little more knowledge of the facts, owing to the defective means of obtaining correct returns.

being *in*sufficient in an estimate of the schools of the poorer classes. Secondly, he includes among them Infant Schools, which do not properly fall within the category of Day Schools at all, and relate chiefly to children not within the age which forms the scope of the calculation. Thirdly, he couples an estimate of scholars with an estimate of the amount of school accommodation, adding them together and taking credit for the latter precisely as for the former. Fourthly, this estimate of school accommodation since 1833 is exaggerated, and comprises, as before, *Infant* Schools. It is safe to say that the conclusion is widely above the truth and utterly without effect or bearing upon the question.* Nor would it have been worth while to have noticed these mis-calculations at all, but for the fact that, strange to say, they are, I believe, the latest estimate which has been put forth on the subject, and has obtained some degree of credence.

---

* For fuller details of these mistakes, see *A Plea for Schools*. Ridgway, 1847.

APPENDIX B.

CRIMINAL OFFENCES DURING 1848, 1849, AND 1850, COMPARED
WITH POPULATION, ETC.

COUNTIES.	Population in 1851.	Persons to each 100 acres.	CRIMINAL OFFENCES.			CRIMINAL OFFENCES, in each 1000 Persons.			Per Centage signing Register with Marks in 1848.
			* Grave.	* Minor.	Total.	Grave	Minor	Total	
Beds . . .	129,789	43	85	442	527	·65	3·40		52·6
Berks . .	199,154	41	170	866	1036	·85	4·34		41·5
Bucks . .	143,670	31	137	702	839	·95	4·88		49·2
Camb. . .	191,856	35	129	726	855	·67	3·78		44·7
Chesh. . .	423,438	65	408	2423	2831	·96	5·72		44·5
Cornw. . .	356,662	42	152	623	775	·42	1·74		42·2
Cumb. . .	195,487	20	63	372	435	·32	1·90		23·3
Derby . .	260,707	40	117	647	764	·44	2·48		35·9
Devon . .	572,207	34	277	2347	2624	·48	4·10		31·7
Dorset . .	177,597	29	96	707	803	·54	3·98		36·9
Durh. . .	411,532	62	166	847	1013	·40	2·05		36·4
Essex . .	343,916	34	298	1609	1907	·86	4·67		47·1
Glouc. . .	419,475	53	360	2665	3025	·85	6·35		33·2
Heref. . .	99,112	18	129	635	764	1·30	6·40		41·0
Herts . .	173,963	43	144	837	981	·82	4·81		50·6
Hunts . .	60,320	25	40	247	287	·66	4·09		45·0
Kent . .	619,207	63	456	2502	2958	·73	4·04		56·8
Lanc. . .	2,063,913	200	1440	8968	10,408	·60	4·34		50·3
Leic. . . .	234,938	45	112	833	945	·47	3·54		38·6
Linc. . .	400,266	23	190	1371	1561	·47	3·42		38·0
Middx. . .	1,895,710	1,059	1,629	10,820	12,449	·85	5·70		33·0
Monm. . .	177,165	55	177	924	1101	·99	5·21		56·5
Norf. . .	433,803	33	252	1775	2027	·58	4·09		44·3
Northam. .	213,784	33	132	750	882	·61	3·50		40·9
Northumb. .	303,535	26	175	570	745	·57	1·87		29·1
Notts . .	294,438	55	121	909	1030	·41	3·08		40·2
Oxon . .	170,286	37	105	746	851	·61	4·38		36·1
Rutl. . .	24,272	25	23	91	114	·94	3·74		29.8
Salop . .	245,019	28	146	813	959	·59	3·31		48·8
Somers . .	456,237	43	397	2130	2527	·87	4·66		36·9
South. . .	402,033	38	247	1918	2165	·61	4·77		36·6
Stafford . .	630,506	83	455	2727	3182	·72	4·32		51·6
Suff. . .	335,991	37	194	1310	1504	·57	3·89		46·1
Surrey . .	684,805	144	524	2911	3435	·76	4·25		37·8
Sussex . .	339,428	37	201	1327	1528	·59	3·90		33·1
Warw. . .	479,979	83	469	2578	3047	·97	5·37		36·7
Westm. . .	58,380	12	20	154	174	·34	2·63		17·2
Wilts . .	241,003	28	169	1134	1303	·70	4·70		45·1
Worc. . .	258,762	55	321	1620	1941	1·24	6·26		42·3
York . .	1,788,767	49	1053	4920	5973	·58	2·75		42·0
Wales, N. .	404,160	20	182	804	986	·45	1·98		55·6
Wales, S. .	607,496	22	267	1450	1717	·43	2·38		55·2
Totals & Averages }	17,922,768	48	12,228	72,750	84,978	·67	4·05	4·74	38·31

* The *grave* offences consist of offences against the person, and offences against property committed with violence.

The *minor* offences are mainly offences against property *without* violence; and also all malicious offences against property, forgery, and all other offences tried at assizes and sessions.

APPENDIX C.

SCRIPTURE PROOFS AND PRECEPTS.

No. 1.

God's Attributes.

GOD'S GREATNESS and OMNIPRESENCE.—One God and Father of all, who is above all, and through all, and in you all. *Ephes.* iv. 6.

In the Lord Jehovah is everlasting strength. *Isa.* xxvi. 4.

HIS OMNISCIENCE.—God is greater than your heart, and knoweth all things. 1 *John* iii. 20.

Thine eyes are open upon all the ways of the sons of men. *Jer.* xxxii. 19.

HIS JUSTICE.—A God of truth and without iniquity, just and right is he. *Deut.* xxxii. 4.

HIS LOVE AND MERCY.—God so loved the world, that he gave his only begotten Son, that whosoever believeth in him should not perish, but have everlasting life. *John* iii. 16.

Greater love hath no man than this, that a man lay down his life for his friends. *John* xv. 13.

For he is gracious and merciful, slow to anger, and of great kindness, and repenteth him of the evil. *Joel* ii. 13.

HIS FAITHFULNESS.—The Lord is faithful, who shall stablish you, and keep you from evil. 2 *Thess.* iii. 3.

The Principles of Salvation.

OUR SINFUL NATURE.—We were by nature the children of wrath. *Ephes.* ii. 3.

The natural man receiveth not the things of the Spirit of God. 1 *Cor.* ii. 14.

All have sinned. *Rom.* v. 12.

I was shapen in iniquity, and in sin did my mother conceive me. *Psalm* li. 5.

THE PUNISHMENT OF SIN.—The wages of sin is death, but the gift of God is eternal life through Jesus Christ our Lord. *Rom.* vi. 23.

SALVATION OFFERED TO ALL.—Whosoever will, let him take of the water of life freely. *Rev.* xxii. 17.

For God hath not appointed us to wrath, but to obtain salvation by our Lord Jesus Christ. 1 *Thess.* v. 9.

Whosoever shall call upon the name of the Lord shall be saved. *Rom.* x. 13.

And he is the propitiation for our sins : and not for ours only, but also for the sins of the whole world. 1 *John* ii. 2.

Parable.—The Marriage Supper. *Luke* xiv. 16.

CHRIST, SOLE MEANS OF SALVATION.—I determined not to know anything among you, save Jesus Christ, and him crucified. 1 *Cor.* ii. 2.

I am the way, and the truth, and the life : no man cometh unto the Father, but by me. *John* xiv. 6.

For other foundation can no man lay than that is laid, which is Jesus Christ. 1 *Cor.* iii. 11.

Parable.—The Vine and the Branches. *John* xv. 1.

THE ATONEMENT BY CHRIST.—For he is our peace, who hath made both one, and hath broken down the middle wall of partition between us; and that he might reconcile both unto God in one body by the cross, having slain the enmity thereby. *Ephes.* ii. 14 and 16.

We also joy in God through our Lord Jesus Christ, by whom we have now received the atonement. *Rom.* v. 11.

We are bought with a price. 1 *Cor.* vii. 23.

GRACE.—For by grace are ye saved through faith; and that not of yourselves : it is the gift of God : not of works, lest any man should boast. *Ephes.* ii. 8.

My grace is sufficient for thee; for my strength is made perfect in weakness. 2 *Cor.* xii. 9.

FAITH.—Without faith it is impossible to please God. *Heb.* xi. 6.

Whosoever believeth in him should not perish, but have eternal life. *John* iii. 15.

He that believeth on me shall never thirst. *John* vi. 35.

He that believeth on me hath everlasting life. *John* vi. 47

Parable.—The Wedding Garment. *Matt.* xxii. 11.

Duties.

BROTHERLY LOVE.—Love is the fulfilling of the law. *Rom.* xiii. 10.

A new commandment give I unto you, That ye love one another; as I have loved you, that ye also love one another. By this shall all men know that ye are my disciples, if ye have love one to another. *John* xiii. 34, 35.

Love as brethren. 1 *Peter* iii. 8.

Bear ye one another's burdens, and so fulfil the law of Christ. *Gal.* vi. 2.

CHARITY.—Above all these things put on charity, which is the bond of perfectness. *Col.* iii. 14.

He that hath pity upon the poor lendeth unto the Lord; and that which he hath given will he pay him again. *Prov.* xix. 17.

Blessed is he that considereth the poor; the Lord will deliver him in time of trouble. *Psalm* xli. 1.

FORGIVENESS OF INJURIES.—If ye forgive not men their trespasses, neither will your Father forgive your trespasses. *Matt.* vi. 15.

Love your enemies, bless them that curse you, do good to them that hate you, and pray for them which despitefully use you, and persecute you. *Matt.* v. 44.

Parables.—The Good Samaritan. *Luke* x. 25. The Unmerciful Servant. *Matt.* xviii. 23.

GENTLENESS.—The servant of the Lord must not strive; but be gentle unto all men, apt to teach, patient. 2 *Tim.* ii. 24.

WATCHFULNESS.—Watch therefore, for ye know neither the day nor the hour wherein the Son of Man cometh. *Matt.* xxv. 13.

The day of the Lord so cometh as a thief in the night. 1 *Thess.* v. 2.

Therefore let us not sleep as do others, but let us watch and be sober. 1 *Thess.* v. 6.

Parable.—The Ten Virgins. *Matt.* xxv. 1.

REPENTANCE.—Repent ye therefore and be converted, that your sins may be blotted out. *Acts* iii. 19.

I say unto you, that likewise joy shall be in heaven over one sinner that repenteth, more than over ninety and nine just persons, which need no repentance. *Luke* xv. 7.

Parables.—The Prodigal Son. *Luke* xv. 11. The Barren Fig Tree. *Luke* xiii. 6.

INDUSTRY.—The hand of the diligent maketh rich. *Prov.* x. 4.

This was the iniquity of thy sister Sodom, pride, fulness of bread, and abundance of idleness was in her. *Ezek.* xvi. 49.

Slothfulness casteth into a deep sleep; and an idle soul shall suffer hunger. *Prov.* xix. 15.

Parable.—The Talents. *Matt.* xxv. 14.

USE OF INSTRUCTION.—Whoso loveth instruction, loveth knowledge: but he that hateth reproof is brutish. *Prov.* xii. 1.

Search the Scriptures. *John* v. 39.

Hear counsel, and receive instruction, that thou mayest be wise in the latter end. *Prov.* xix. 20.

Fools hate knowledge. *Prov.* i. 22.

Parable.—The Sower and the Seed. *Matt.* xiii. 18.

TRUTHFULNESS.—Lying lips are abomination to the Lord; but they that deal truly are his delight. *Prov.* xii. 22.

Wherefore putting away lying, speak every man truth with his neighbour: for we are members one of another. *Ephes.* iv. 25.

PRAYER.—Watch ye therefore, and pray always. *Luke* xxi. 36.

Watch and pray, that ye enter not into temptation. *Matt.* xxvi. 41.

Parable.—The Importunate Widow. *Luke* xviii. 1.

LOVE OF THE WORLD.—What shall it profit a man, if he shall gain the whole world, and lose his own soul? *Mark* viii. 36.

Set your affections on things above, not on things on the earth. *Col.* iii. 2.

Parable.—Dives and Lazarus. *Luke* xvi. 19—26.

OBEDIENCE.—Children, obey your parents in the Lord, for this is right. *Ephes.* vi. 1.

Obey them that have the rule over you, and submit yourselves. *Heb.* xiii. 17.

See the Fifth Commandment.

HUMILITY.—He that trusteth in his own heart is a fool. *Prov.* xxviii. 26.

Whosoever shall not receive the kingdom of God as a little child shall in no wise enter therein. *Luke* xviii. 17.

Humble yourselves therefore under the mighty hand of God, that he may exalt you in due time. 1 *Peter* v. 6.

Whosoever exalteth himself shall be abased; and he that humbleth himself shall be exalted. *Luke* xiv. 11.

Parables.—The Wedding Rooms. *Luke* xiv. 8. The Pharisee and Publican. *Luke* xviii. 10.

GOOD WORKS.—If ye love me, keep my commandments. *John* xiv. 15.

He that saith, I know him, and keepeth not his commandments, is a liar, and the truth is not in him. But whoso keepeth his word, in him verily is the love of God perfected: hereby know we that we are in him. 1 *John* ii. 4, 5.

Even so faith, if it hath not works, is dead, being alone. *James* ii. 17.

Parable.—The Barren Fig Tree. *Luke* xiii. 6.

SCRIPTURE PROOFS AND PRECEPTS.
No. 2.
Trinity.

Go ye therefore, and teach all nations, baptizing them in the name of the Father, and of the Son, and of the Holy Ghost. *Matt.* xxviii. 19.

The grace of the Lord Jesus Christ, and the love of God, and the communion of the Holy Ghost, be with you all. 2 *Cor.* xiii. 14.

Divinity of Christ.

Unto us a child is born, unto us a son is given, and the government shall be upon his shoulder : and his name shall be called Wonderful, Counsellor, The mighty God, The everlasting Father, The Prince of Peace. *Isaiah* ix. 6.

And this is his name whereby he shall be called, THE LORD OUR RIGHTEOUSNESS. *Jer.* xxiii. 6.

In the beginning was the Word, and the Word was with God, and the Word was God. *John* i. 1.

In him dwelleth all the fulness of the Godhead bodily. *Col.* ii. 9.

Without controversy, great is the mystery of godliness : God was manifest in the flesh, justified in the Spirit, seen of angels, preached unto the Gentiles, believed on in the world, received up into glory. 1 *Tim.* iii. 16.

But unto the Son he saith, Thy throne, O God, is for ever and ever. *Heb.* i. 8.

Divinity of the Holy Ghost.

The Spirit of God moved upon the face of the waters. *Gen.* i. 2.

The Lord God and his Spirit hath sent me. *Isaiah* xlviii. 16.

The Holy Ghost shall come upon thee, and the power of the Highest shall overshadow thee : therefore also that holy thing which shall be born of thee shall be called the Son of God. *Luke* i. 35.

Why hath Satan filled thine heart to lie to the Holy Ghost?
*   *   Thou hast not lied unto men, but unto God. *Acts* v. 3, 4.

The Lord is that Spirit. 2 *Cor.* iii. 17.

The Holy Ghost proceedeth from the Father and the Son.

When the Comforter is come, whom I will send unto you from the Father, even the Spirit of Truth, which proceedeth from the Father, he shall testify of me. *John* xv. 26.

Because ye are sons, God hath sent forth the Spirit of his Son into your hearts, crying, Abba, Father. *Gal.* iv. 6.

Searching what, or what manner of time the Spirit of Christ which was in them did signify, when it testified beforehand the sufferings of Christ and the glory that should follow. 1 *Peter* i. 11.

Attributes of the Holy Ghost.

HE GIVES LIFE.—The Spirit is life. *Rom.* viii. 10.
It is the Spirit that quickeneth. *John* vi. 63.

HE IS OMNIPRESENT.—Whither shall I go from thy Spirit? or whither shall I flee from thy presence? If I ascend up into heaven, thou art there; if I make my bed in hell, behold, thou art there. *Ps.* cxxxix. 7, 8.

HE IS ETERNAL.—Who through the eternal Spirit offered himself without spot to God. *Heb.* ix. 14.

HE IS ETERNAL.—The Spirit searcheth all things, yea, the deep things of God. 1 *Cor.* ii. 10.

HE IS FAITHFUL AND TRUE.—It is the Spirit that beareth witness, because the Spirit is truth. 1 *John* v. 6.

HE IS HOLY.—Take not thy Holy Spirit from me. *Psalm* li. 11.
Grieve not the holy Spirit of God. *Ephes.* iv. 30.

HE IS LOVING.—The Comforter, which is the Holy Ghost. *John* xiv. 26.
The love of God is shed abroad in our hearts by the Holy Ghost which he hath given us. *Rom.* v. 5.

Operations and Gifts of the Holy Ghost.

HEAVENLY WISDOM.—He shall teach you all things, and bring all things to your remembrance whatsoever I have said unto you. *John* xiv. 26.

No man can say that Jesus is the Lord, but by the Holy Ghost. 1 *Cor.* xii. 3.

And the Spirit of the Lord shall rest upon him, the spirit of wisdom and understanding, the spirit of council and might, the spirit of knowledge and of the fear of the Lord. *Isaiah* xi. 2.

The things of God knoweth no man, but the Spirit of God. 1 *Cor.* ii. 11.

REGENERATION.—That which is born of the Spirit is spirit. *John* iii. 6.

JUSTIFICATION.—And such were some of you; but ye are washed, but ye are sanctified, but ye are justified, in the name of the Lord Jesus, and by the Spirit of our God. 1 *Cor.* vi. 11.

SANCTIFICATION.—God hath from the beginning chosen you to salvation through sanctification of the Spirit and belief of the truth. 2 *Thess.* ii. 13.

The fruit of the Spirit is in all goodness, and righteousness, and truth. *Ephes.* v. 9.

The fruit of the Spirit is love, joy, peace, long suffering, gentleness, goodness, faith, meekness, temperance. *Gal.* v. 22.

ADOPTION.—As many as are led by the Spirit of God, they are the sons of God. For ye have not received the spirit of bondage again to fear; but ye have received the Spirit of adoption, whereby we cry, Abba, Father. The Spirit itself beareth witness with our spirit that we are the children of God. *Rom.* viii. 14—16.

Extraordinary Operations of the Holy Spirit.

INSPIRATION.—The sword of the Spirit, which is the word of God. *Ephes.* vi. 17.

The prophecy came not in old time by the will of man; but holy men of God spake as they were moved by the Holy Ghost. 2 *Peter* i. 21.

MIRACULOUS POWERS.—To another the gifts of healing by the same spirit; to another the working of miracles; to another prophecy; to another discerning of spirits; to another divers kinds of tongues; to another the interpretation of tongues. 1 *Cor.* xii. 9, 10.

KNOWLEDGE OF FUTURITY.—And the Holy Ghost was upon him; and it was revealed unto him by the Holy Ghost that he should not see death, before he had seen the Lord's Christ. *Luke* ii. 25, 26.

Unity of God.

Hear, O Israel, the Lord our God is one Lord. *Deut.* vi. 4.

To us there is but one God, the Father, of whom are all things, and we in him; and one Lord Jesus Christ, by whom are all things, and we by him. 1 *Cor.* viii. 6.

One Lord, one faith, one baptism, one God and Father of all. *Ephes.* iv. 5, 6.

See also the First and Second Commandments.

The Atonement.

He was wounded for our transgressions, he was bruised for our iniquities; the chastisement of our peace was upon him, and with his stripes we are healed. The Lord hath laid on him the iniquity of us all. He was cut off out of the land of the living: for the transgression of my people was he stricken. *Isaiah* liii. 5, 6, 7.

Behold the Lamb of God, which taketh away the sin of the world. *John* i. 29.

The blood of Jesus Christ his Son cleanseth us from all sin. 1 *John* i. 7.

Christ our Passover is sacrificed for us. 1 *Cor.* v. 7.

Christ was once offered to bear the sins of many. *Heb.* ix. 28.

Christ hath redeemed us from the curse of the law, being made a curse for us. *Gal.* iii. 13.

Christ's Mediation and Intercession.

Being justified by faith, we have peace with God through our Lord Jesus Christ; by whom also we have access by faith into this grace wherein we stand, and rejoice in hope of the glory of God. *Rom.* v. 1, 2.

Whatsoever ye shall ask the Father in my name, he will give it you. *John* xvi. 23.

He is the Mediator of the New Testament. *Heb.* ix. 15.

There is one God, and one Mediator between God and man, the man Christ Jesus. 1 *Tim.* ii. 5.

If any man sin, we have an Advocate with the Father, Jesus Christ the righteous. 1 *John* ii. 1.

He bare the sin of many, and made intercession for the transgressors. *Isaiah* liii. 12.

Wherefore he is able to save them to the uttermost that come unto God by him, seeing he ever liveth to make intercession for them. *Heb.* vii. 25.

Holy Spirit's Intercession.

Likewise the Spirit also helpeth our infirmities, for we know not what we should pray for as we ought, but the Spirit itself maketh intercession for us with groanings which cannot be uttered. And he that searcheth the hearts knoweth what is the mind of the Spirit, because he maketh intercession for the saints according to the will of God. *Rom.* viii. 26, 27.

Prayer in the Name of Jesus.

Whatsoever ye shall ask in my name, that will I do, that the Father may be glorified in the Son. If ye shall ask anything in my name, I will do it. *John* xiv. 13, 14.

Giving thanks always for all things unto God and the Father in the name of our Lord Jesus Christ. *Ephes.* v. 20.

Social and Public Worship.

Again I say unto you, that if two of you shall agree on earth, as touching anything that they shall ask, it shall be done for them of my Father which is in heaven. For where two or three are gathered together in my name, there am I in the midst of them. *Matt.* xviii. 19, 20.

Not forsaking the assembling of ourselves together, as the manner of some is, but exhorting one another. *Heb.* x. 25.

The Sacraments.

BAPTISM.—Verily, verily, I say unto thee, Except a man be born of water and of the Spirit, he cannot enter into the kingdom of God. *John* iii. 5.

Go ye, therefore, and teach all nations, baptizing them in the name of the Father, and of the Son, and of the Holy Ghost. *Matt.* xxviii. 19.

LORD'S SUPPER.—And he took bread, and gave thanks, and brake it, and gave unto them, saying, This is my body, which is given for you: this do in remembrance of me. Likewise also the cup after supper, saying, This cup is the new Testament in my blood, which is shed for you. *Luke* xxii. 19, 20.

As often as ye eat this bread and drink this cup, ye do show the Lord's death till he come. 1 *Cor.* xi. 26.

Duties.

KEEPING THE SABBATH.—Ye shall keep my sabbaths, and reverence my sanctuary: I am the Lord. *Lev.* xix. 30.

See also the Fourth Commandment.

ABSTINENCE FROM PROFANE SWEARING.—Above all things, my brethren, swear not: neither by heaven, neither by the earth, neither by any other oath; but let your yea be yea, and your nay, nay, lest ye fall into condemnation. *James* v. 12.

Bless them which persecute you: bless and curse not. *Rom.* xii. 14.

TEMPERANCE.—Every man that striveth for the mastery is temperate in all things. I keep under my body and bring it into subjection, lest that by any means, when I have preached to others, I myself should be a castaway. 1 *Cor.* ix. 25, 27.

SOBRIETY.—Look not upon the wine when it is red, when it giveth his colour in the cup, when it moveth itself aright. At the last it biteth like a serpent, and stingeth like an adder. *Proverbs* xxiii. 31, 32.

CHASTITY.—Flee fornication. 1 *Cor.* vi. 18.

Whoremongers and adulterers God will judge. *Heb.* xiii. 4.

HONESTY.—Render therefore unto all their dues. Owe no man anything, but to love one another. *Rom.* xiii. 7, 8.

The Final Judgment.

The wages of sin is death; but the gift of God is eternal life through Jesus Christ our Lord. *Rom.* vi. 23.

APPENDIX D.

PRODUCE OF FIELD GARDENING.

MARKET DRAYTON.

19th March, 1851.

In answer to your letter of the 17th instant, I am sorry it is not in my power to give you the exact account of the time, and the number of the men and boys employed in the cultivation of our small spot of land. We have very rarely in the summer time more than two or three old men that are able to do anything in the garden, so that I am obliged to use the boys for what is done, and as our garden has always a crop on it the labour is very light, and is done as the land becomes vacant. The produce has not made so much in money value this year as usual, in consequence of the prejudice raised in the Staffordshire potteries at the time of the cholera against the consumption of cabbage, and it is on that market that the people of Market Drayton depend for the sale of their garden produce; so that I was forced to sell at 3*d*. per dozen, what I had used to sell at 6*d*. or 7*d*. a dozen; in fact, I sold more last year for 7*l*. 15*s*. 8½*d*., than I did the year before for 16*l*., and the crops occupied the land longer for the smaller sum than they did for the larger one. My garden looks extremely well at this time; it is all set but one small flat, which I intend to sow to-morrow (if the weather be fine), and has only one fault, which is being too full of manure, and yet I have some thousands of gallons of liquid manure that I do not know what to do with. I am happy to inform you that the Guardians have purchased upwards of five acres of common land to erect a new workhouse upon, which will give us a good opportunity for training the children to habits of industry, the employment of such of the old men as are able to do a little, as well as afford an opportunity for making the best of all the refuse that is unavoidably caused by a large family; in fact I shall rigidly endeavour to apply the precept ' Gather up the crumbs, that nothing be lost,' to all that comes under my care; for I have long been convinced that no person *ought* to waste anything that can be turned to a profitable account, but what they can *create themselves;* and we all ought to consider that one atom wasted has a tendency to produce scarcity, which ultimately falls with the greatest severity upon the poor of the land, who are the least able to bear it; and yet unfortunately, from the want of a better education, the poor are the greatest wasters. Below is a statement of the proceeds of 3½ roods 15 poles of land, for the last year, under the most unfavourable circumstances.

	£	s.	d.
Vegetables consumed in the house 12,488 lbs. at 20*d*. per 90 lbs., being rated at about 2*s*. 3*d*., the value of potatoes in this neighbourhood	11	11	3
Sold vegetables for	7	15	8¼
The value of onions, thyme, parsley, mint, peas, carrots. &c.	8	0	0
I consider that about ⅕ of the garden produce is wasted from the want of the better means of consumption, which, being reckoned at half the price of the other vegetables, would give $\frac{19\ 6\ 11\frac{1}{4}}{12}$	1	12	2½
Total produce for the last year	28	19	2
To which add	8	4	3½
The produce of the last year but one	37	3	5½

HEREFORD.

12*th August*, 1850.

1. In answer to your inquiries, I beg to say we have 7 acres of land under spade cultivation. The first crop this year was 2¾ acres vetches, which fed six milking cows through the months May, June, and July. The land is now under the following-named crops :—

	A.	R.	P.
Potatoes.	1	0	0
Mangel-wurzel	3	0	0
Carrots	1	0	0
Parsnips.	0	2	0
Cabbage	0	3	0
Turnips	0	3	0
Total	7	0	0

The whole of the crops are looking well, and give great satisfaction to the Board of Guardians and a host of visitors.

2. The boys I have to work vary from day to day, but I think the average is about 10 boys, age from 7 to 14 years, and one man.

3. I think 6 boys with an overlooker would cultivate two acres of land in the way we do ours.

4. Boys may be profitably employed upon the land at 7 years of age, if healthy and strong, at such work as weeding, hoeing, watering, picking stones, and other light jobs; and I am quite certain boys this way employed will be better able to get their living

at 10 years of age, than those unemployed at 15 or 16 years of age. I know well by my own case; I myself went to work at 7 years of age.   *   *   *   *   *

3rd January, 1851.

The quantity of land under cultivation is seven acres, crop as undermentioned:—2 acres mangold-wurzel, 1½ potatoes, 1 cabbage, 1 carrots, ½ an acre parsnips, 1 turnips. The exact amount, as it stands in the daybook, from January 1, to the end of December, 1850 :—

	£	s.	d.
Butter	54	11	9
Milk	37	3	5
Cheese	7	1	3
3 Fat Cows	37	6	0
6 Calves	14	4	8
8 Pork Pigs	12	17	11
Cabbage	2	1	6
Potatoes	17	16	6
Carrots	3	3	5
Turnips	0	13	8
Total	£187	0	1

The average number of boys per day amount to 8 as near as possible, and men 2 per day. I consider the value of roots on hand to be as follows :—Carrots, 5l.; wurzel, 10l.; turnips, 5l.; potatoes, 8l. 16s.; Total 28l. 16s. We have 7 cows on the land; the value of them, according to Mr. Racsters' valuation, would be 77l., and 9 pigs, worth 18l. There is growing one acre of winter vetches worth 5l. The Italian rye-grass I can say but little about, but it appears well, and I have no doubt as to trial of it proving favourable. I have spared no pain to answer your inquiries correct.

PEMBROKE.

17th August, 1850.

1. The only parts capable of being cropped systematically of our land are about 4484 square yards.

2. We average 12 boys in the house between the ages of 8 and 13, who, under the superintendence of the schoolmaster, do all the work without any other assistance. Indeed, I could work the ground fairly with half the number of boys.

3. About 8 boys would be sufficient.

4. About 7 years of age, and perhaps in setting wheat, beans, potatoes, &c., after dibblers; picking stones, and cleaning the offal, weeds, rubbish, &c., better than older boys.

11th January, 1851.

The extent of the ground under cultivation is nearly one and three quarters of an acre, upon which wheat, vetches, swedish turnips, cabbages, potatoes, carrots, mangold-wurzel, and other small seeds are grown.

The number of boys above nine years old employed in the cultivation of this ground has not averaged more than ten; they have not received any assistence from the old men, excepting about one week in the spring of the year, when the small seed and other work in the kitchen garden required it. I have no able-bodied men in the house, and only eight old men; four only of them are capable of being employed in this work; two are generally splitting wood, making balls (our country firing), breaking stones, cutting straw, and such small matters as they are capable of doing; one acts as gatekeeper, while the other is employed as a messenger; but they are all aged and very infirm. The piece under wheat consisted of 1216 square yards, upon which I caused six and a quarter pints of seed to be dibbled in, in rows of nine inches asunder, and six inches between the plants; it produced 457 lbs., and was sold at 6s. per Winchester of 62 lbs., producing 2l. 4s. 2½d. ¾ of a Winchester of vetches was sown upon 1522 square yards; it was cut green and sold to various persons in the town, producing a sum of 2l. 12s. 7½d. This crop was succeeded by one of swedish turnips sown in drills twenty inches asunder, being first well dressed and hand-hoed, leaving the plants ten inches apart: the weight was not ascertained, all having been used in the house, and calculated at six for a penny. I cannot accurately give the extent of ground under cabbages, as I invariably kept filling up every vacant spot when it did not interfere with other crops. I begin to sow the seed in the second week of March, and continue the operation about once a fortnight until August, the final sowing being from the 6th to the 12th of that month, which at the beginning, middle, and latter end of September, are in a fit state to be transplanted into nursery beds to stand the winter and come to plant off early in the spring, producing good cabbage about the end of May or the beginning of June; this crop is accounted for in the balance-sheet at ¼d. per pound. The potatoes occupied 3129 square yards, and the produce was used in the house debited to in-maintenance at 10l. 17s., and credited to establishment.

Belgian and Altringham carrot-seed were sown in 245 square yards, dibbled in rows twelve inches apart, and at a distance of five and a half inches between the plants; the other portions were cropped with onions, leeks, beans, peas, and small seed, all which appear in the balance-sheet, which I have hopes will be satisfactory, and prove that the system carried out here (although upon so small a scale) answers the expectations of its promoters. In the present year there has been an excess of profit on the last by 4l. 12s. 7¾d., while the boys employed have been younger and less in number.

Garden account for the year ending Christmas, 1850.

	Cost of the Seed, &c.				Value of the Produce used in the House.			Value of the Produce sold.		
	£	s.	d.		£	s.	d.	£	s.	d.
Wheat . . .	0	0	8	Wheat . . .		...		2	4	2½
Vetches . . .	0	6	0	Thatch, 300 .	1	10	0	0	1	6
Potatoes . .	3	6	3	Vetches . . .		...		2	12	7½
Small Seed . .	0	18	5	Cabbage plants .		...		0	5	2½
Mangold-wurzel				Potatoes debited						
Seed . . .	0	1	0	to maintenance						
Turnip Seed .	0	0	6½	and credited to						
Carrot Seed .	0	2	0	establishment .	10	17	0		...	
Pigs	2	17	0	Brocoli . . .	0	18	0	0	0	8½
Value of pigs				Cabbage . . .	2	5	9	0	2	11½
brought for-				Lettuce . . .	0	14	9	0	0	10
ward from				Carrots . . .	1	17	4	1	8	6
last year . .	1	3	0	Mangold-wurzel		...		1	16	0
				Turnips . . .	3	5	2		...	
				Beans . . .	0	9	6		...	
				Peas	0	2	0		...	
				Onions . . .	0	12	0		...	
				Leeks . . .	1	10	0		...	
				Pigs		...		5	19	2⅟₇
				Value of pigs						
				not sold . .	1	19	0		...	
	8	14	10½		26	0	6	14	11	9
By profit .	31	17	4½		14	11	9			
	40	12	3		40	12	3			

P.S. The balance of the produce in the ground as described in the balance-sheet for Christmas, 1849, is not accounted for in this statement, as it was consumed in the house before this account was opened.

Westbury-upon-Severn, Vicarage.

(*Land, one-tenth of an Acre.*)

Cabbages (Drumhead), autumn sown; planted four feet apart in the row, and four feet between the rows—264 at 30 lbs. each, viz. :—

	Tons.	Cwts.	Qrs.	lbs.
20 lbs. each of edible stuff	2	7	0	16
10 lbs. each of rough cattle stuff. . .	1	3	2	8
Potatoes (Ashleaf), planted between the rows of Drumheads—448 lbs., or 1½ bags 228 lbs . .	0	4	0	0
Cabbages (Early York), planted between the drum-heads—228, at 1½ lbs. each	0	3	3	12
	3	18	2	8

The manure was dug into the rows, so that the cabbages had the full benefit of it.

Expenses.

	£	s.	d.
Rent, rates, and taxes, £3 per acre—1s. 10d.	0	6	0
Manure	0	15	0
Cabbages, Drumhead (300), 6d. per 100	0	1	6
Cabbages, Early York (300), 6d. per 100	0	1	6
Potato-seed (Ashleaf), home-grown, 6 pecks, at 1s. 6d. per peck	0	9	0
Winter forking and spring digging, 6 days, at 1s. 6d. per day	0	9	0
Moulding up cabbages and potatoes, and getting up potatoes, 3 days, at 1s. 6d. per day	0	4	6
	£2	6	6

Profit.

	£	s.	d.
Drumhead cabbages, edible, 2 tons 7 cwts. 0 qrs. 16 lbs., at 30s. per ton	3	10	6
Drumhead cabbages, cattle stuff, 1 ton 3 cwts. 2 qrs. 8 lbs., at 10 lbs. for 1d.	1	2	0
Ashleaf kidneys, 1½ bags, at £1 per bag	1	10	0
Early York cabbages, 288, at 1d. each.	1	4	0
	7	6	6
Deduct Expenses, as above	2	6	6
Profit on one-tenth of an acre	£5	0	0

Mr. John Sillett, of Kelsall, near Saxmundham, in his evidence before a Committee of the House of Commons* on July 19, 1848, deposed, that from two acres cultivated by the spade, with stall-fed cows, he had realized 74*l*. from the sale of the produce, after supplying his family, consisting of four persons, with milk, bread, potatoes, and vegetables. He stated, moreover, that he calculated his two cows in the year produced him 29*l*.: they ere the Suffolk cow.

GLOUCESTER, 22*nd of* 12*th month*, 1849.

ESTEEMED FRIEND,

In reply to thy inquiry as to the probable produce of good land under high cultivation, I must confess (in common with many others, I presume) that I have seldom taken the trouble to test carefully the produce per acre of my own land. I have, however, in two or three instances, tested it, and certainly with very satisfactory results. The one instance was a crop of mangel-wurzel planted in rows a yard apart, with early potatoes between each row. I sold the potatoes, when dug in June or July, at the rate of 15*l*. per acre, and I found, by carefully weighing two rows of the mangel-wurzel all through the field, that I had thirty-three tons of roots and ten tons of leaves per acre, and as I could have sold the mangel-wurzel at 1*l*. per ton, the gross produce of the land would in that instance have been 48*l*. per acre.

I also tested the weight of the two first cuttings of my Italian rye-grass this last summer, and found the first crop was eighteen tons, and the second was ten tons to the acre. I cut it twice afterwards, but the weather being dry, the crops were comparatively light, and I did not weigh them. The crop was sown in the autumn, after potatoes, and fed off with sheep three separate times through the winter.

With respect to the quantity of provender to be purchased to maintain the stock proposed to be kept on thirty acres, I cannot form any estimate; but my own opinion would be rather in favour of keeping only such a quantum of stock as the land would feed without purchase, and what this would be experience can accurately determine.

I am, very respectfully and sincerely, thy friend,

To Jelinger C. Symons.   SAM. BOWLY.

---

* See *Report of Committee on National Land Campany,* Session 1848, p. 63.

APPENDIX E.

Q. How long have you used whins, or gorse, for cattle, and whether partially or for your whole establishment?

A. Fourteen years this season for dairy cows, fattening cows, and horses.

Q. What animals do you consider it to suit?

A. It equally suits all the above animals. Sheep I have not tried it with. I doubt whether they will easily be got to eat it: they do not like anything which has been much bruised with iron. Whins must be bruised, and my machine is iron.

Q. In what quantities, and whether alone or mixed with other fodder?

A. Not mixed; three bushels and a half per day is sufficient for each cow. I have four and twenty cows in one house; besides the whins, they eat per day one hundred weight of hay and eight bushels of swedish turnips amongst the twenty-four cows; being about four pounds and a half of hay per cow per day, and twenty pounds of swedes per cow per day. On this dairy cows are kept in excellent condition, and the butter is remarkably good; fattening cows will feed fast. When swedes fail or are scarce, I substitute about four pounds of oil cake per day to each cow, and as the fattening cows get forward I increase the quantity of oil cake gradually; the most I give is twelve pounds per day to large cows, and that only for the last month.

Q. By what machinery is it prepared for use?

A. First cut through a common chaff cutter, then bruised in a mill similar to the old cider mill; the revolving wheel surrounded with fluted iron; at the bottom of the chase a plain iron plate.

Q. In what manner is it cultivated, and at what age, and in what manner cut for use, with the average produce?

A. Sown as clover seed, with a crop of barley or oats—is fit to cut the November twelve months after sowing; it is then mown every year during the winter, as wanted, with a common scythe close to the ground; on good dry land will cut from seven to ten tons per acre.

Q. Is the plant you use the common whins, or gorse, or any particular variety of it?

A. It is called French furze, but is very common in England.

Q. On what do you grow it?

A. On an old woodland, stocked up, part a burning gravel, part a strong clay, but very dry at bottom, and very hilly. Half an acre of this land is on the average sufficient to keep a cow twenty weeks. On rich loomy dry land I have no doubt nearly double quantity may be grown.

Q. What do you consider the peculiar advantage, and what the danger of using it?

A. The advantages are apparent from the above answers. The is no danger in using it if well ground, and mixed with salt in the proportion of four ounces per cow per day.

Q. State the expense of cutting in the field and bruising for use?

A. Mowing, carting, cutting, and bruising, cost not quite a penny a bushel.

Q. State any general observations on the subject.

A. It requires no manure, but in its consumption creates a great deal. Will grow on poor hilly land, if dry, which will not pay for cultivating. When once sown and well rooted, it yields a great quantity of food for cattle at no other expense but the one above stated. I have cut the same ground now for fourteen years —have done nothing to it, and, with the exception of some parts of the burning gravel which the hot weather has this year affected, it seems to promise as good a crop as heretofore. I generally begin to mow it as soon as grass is gone, and it lasts till grass comes again. If there is an appearance of snow, I mow some quantity before hand, and it will keep thrown down in heaps in the rick-yard; but it must not be bruised till it is wanted, as it will not keep after bruising. The quantity of seed to be sown per acre, is twenty pounds. Mine is sown broad cast, but I should recommend it to be drilled as near in the rows as will admit hand-hoeing for the first year or two, if the land is inclined to run to grass. I do not feed with furze on a Sunday, as the cows do not like it unless it is given them fresh from the mill.

RICHARD SPOONER.

APPENDIX F.

GLOUCESTER RAGGED SCHOOL.

At a meeting of some friends of education, held this day, it was resolved that it is expedient to establish a ragged school for boys in this city, on the following principles :—

1st. That the object of the school be to afford practical, religious, and secular instruction to children above the age of six years, of the most destitute class, and who are now without the means of education.

2nd. That the Holy Scriptures be read and explained daily.

3rd. That industrial training be a main feature in the system pursued.

4th. That a suitable house, or rooms, be rented, in or near the island, for the school; and that about four acres of land be also taken near the city, for teaching the elder boys spade husbandry.

5. That the school hours be from nine to half-past twelve daily; at which time the elder boys only (not exceeding forty in number) be supplied with a plain dinner, according to the dietary of the Union Workhouse ; and that these boys comprise the working staff for the cultivation of the ground.

6th. That the working staff of boys be employed in the grounds five days in each week (weather permitting), between the hours of half-past one and five o'clock ; indoor employment being provided for them when prevented from working on the land.

7th. That the ground be cultivated as a vegetable garden ; the produce, after supplying the boys' dinners, to be disposed of in aid of the funds of the establishment.

8th. That the entire control of the school be vested in a committee, to be annually elected by subscribers of 1l. and donors of 10l., in whom the power of making new laws shall be vested, at special meetings summoned for that purpose.

9th. That there be an annual meeting of all subscribers and donors, at which a report of the proceedings of the year shall be read.

10th. That the school be conducted by a school-master who shall be thoroughly competent to teach and train according to the system of the Ragged School Union, and to undertake the entire management of the ground.

11th. That as soon as the funds permit, arrangements be made for extending the benefits of the school to girls, who, in addition to mental instruction in the morning, shall be taught needlework and knitting in the afternoon, by a competent school-mistress; who shall also have the charge of the younger boys, and employ them in some suitable work at the same time.

12th. That the school be supported by voluntary contributions, aided by a grant from the Lords of the Committee of Council.

Gloucester, 24th March, 1851.

DATE DUE

APR 10 1993			